Short Sketches of SAINTS Known & Unknown

J. P. Vaswani

Sterling Paperbacks

Books and Booklets By J.P. Vaswani

In English:
The Seven Commandments of the Bhagavad Gita
Kill Fear Before Fear Kills You
Swallow Irritation Before Irritation Swallows You
Its All A Matter of Attitude
You Can Make A Difference
101 Stories For You and Me
108 Pearls of Practical Wisdom
108 Simple Prayers of A Simple Man
108 Thoughts on Success
114 Thoughts on Love
A Child of God
A Day with Dadaji
A Mystic of Modern India
Begin the Day with God
Beloved Dadaji
Conversations with Dadaji
Dada Answers
Daily Appointment With God
Daily Inspiration
Doors of Heaven
Education: What India Needs
Feast of Love
Five Fragrant Flowers
From Darkness Into Light
From Hell to Heaven
Glimpses
Glimpses Into Great Lives
God In Quest of Man
Hinduism
How to Have Real Fun Out of Life and other Talks
How to Make Your Life A Love Story
How to Overcome Temptations
How to Overcome Tensions
I Have Need of You
I Luv U, God!
Invest in the Child
Joy Peace Pills
Laugh Your Way to Health
Life After Death
Life is A Love Story
Love and Laugh!
Nestle Now
Notes from the Master's Lute
Pictures and Parables
Positive Power of Thanksgiving
Prayers of A Pilgrim
Prophets and Patriots
Sadhu Vaswani: His Life and Teachings
Little Lamps
Secrets of Health and Happiness

Shanti Speaks
Snacks for the Soul
More Snacks for the Soul
Stories for Meditation
Stories for You and Me
Teach Me to Pray
Tear-Drops (poems)
Temple Flowers
Ten Commandents of A Successful Marriage
The Holy Man of Hyderabad
The Kingdom of Krishna
A Little Book of Life
A Little Book of Wisdom
The Little Book of Prayer
The Little Book of Service
The Little Book of Success
The Little Book of Yoga
The Little Book of Freedom From Stress
The Magic of Forgiveness
The Simple Way
The Story of A Simple Man
The Way of *Abhyasa* (How to Meditate)
Ticket to Heaven
Twinkle, Twinkle Tiny Star
What You Would Like to Know about *Karma*
Whispers
Why Do Good People Suffer?
You Are Not Alone!
You Can Be A Smile Millionaire
Destination Happiness
Ladder of *Abhyasa*
Peace or Perish – There is no Other Choice
Good Parenting
Teachers Are Sculptors
I am a Sindhi
The Perfect Relationship: *Guru and Disciple*

In Hindi:

Ishwar Tujhe Pranaam
Prarthna Ki Shakti
Alwar Santon Ki Mahaan Gaathaayein
Atmik Jalpaan
Atmik Poshan
Bhale Logon Ke Saath Bura Kyon
Chitra Darshan
Dainik Prerna
Krodh Ko Jalayen, Swayam Ko Nahi
Mahan Purush Jeevan Darshan
Santon Ki Lila
Mrityun Hai Dwaar Phir Kya
Safal Vivah Ka Dus Rahasya

Published by
Sterling Publishers Private Limited

STERLING PAPERBACKS
An imprint of
Sterling Publishers (P) Ltd.
A-59, Okhla Industrial Area, Phase-II,
New Delhi-110020.
Tel: 26387070, 26386209; Fax: 91-11-26383788
E-mail: sterlingpublishers@airtelmail.in
ghai@nde.vsnl.net.in
www.sterlingpublishers.com

Short Sketches of Saints: Known & Unknown
© 2008, J. P. Vaswani
ISBN 978 81 207 3999 4

All rights are reserved.
No part of this publication may be reproduced, stored in a retrieval system or transmitted, in any form or by any means, mechanical, photocopying, recording or otherwise, without prior written permission of the author.

Printed and Published by Sterling Publishers Pvt. Ltd.,
New Delhi-110 020.

Contents

Gautama Buddha 1
Sant Tulsidas 18
Guru Nanak 31
Sri Ramakrishna Paramahansa 45
Baha'u'llah 59
Lord Dattatreya 69
Helen Keller 87
Leo Tolstoy 97
Rabiya 106
Toyohiko Kagawa 119
Jamshed Nusserwanji 130
Ibrahim Ibn Adham 137

Latif Shah	150
Ma Saradamani	157
Guru Gobind Singh	169
Durgacharan Nag	180
Dharam Devi	200
Bhakta Ramdas	208
Sant Purandardas	219
Swami Ugradas	229

Gautama Buddha

Gautama, the Buddha, was one of India's great gifts to the world and its civilisation. Millions all over the world call themselves Buddhists and draw inspiration from the life and the work of Buddha. Through precept and practice he taught that one of the highest values in life is *maitreyi,* love for all, fellowship with the poor and lowly. Buddha recognised no caste. He recognised the sacred claims of all humanity, all life. Buddha taught that *bodhi,* wisdom was open to all, the poorest of the poor, the humblest of the humble.

Gautama Buddha

Wherever you turn, in this world of ours, you find misery and sorrow. Unhappiness is writ on every face you see. Everyone is in search of true lasting joy and peace. Alas, very few find what they seek!

Let us reflect on the life of one who found the way to this lasting peace.

The Buddha was born over two thousand five hundred years ago, as the son of a king – Raja Suddhodhana. He was born on the sacred day of Vaisakh Purnima at Lumbini, situated near the city of Kapilavastu. Seven days after his birth, his mother Maya passed away. The child was therefore, brought up under the care of Maya's sister, Prajapati. The royal astrologer prophesied that the infant, whom they named Siddhartha, would grow to be either a great *Chakravarti* (an Emperor) or a renunciate who would bring inner enlightenment to thousands of lost souls. The father surrounded the Prince with luxuries and comforts. But the thought of world-sorrow entered his heart. There is suffering when man is born: there is suffering when he falls sick: there is suffering when he dies. Is there no way out of the world's sorrow?

The father was always anxious lest his son should renounce the palace and become a hermit. Siddhartha told his father, "If you, beloved father, assure me of three things, I shall never leave your palace." The king asked his son what those three things were. The prince replied, "The first thing is that I shall never fall sick. Secondly, that I will never become old. Thirdly, that I shall never die. Death should never touch me."

The King was perplexed. How could he assure Siddhartha of these things? "Look at me," he said to his son, "every now and then, I keep falling sick; how can I assure you then, that you will not fall sick? Wrinkles are writ on my face, my hair has turned grey; how then, can I promise you that you will never grow old? The law of this world is that one who is born must die. How can I then assure you of immortality?" Then said the prince, "I shall set out in quest of a cure to the misery, sorrow and suffering of human life!"

To keep him bound, Raja Suddhodhana got him married to one of the most beautiful girls of the realm – Princess Yashodhara, the daughter of the Koliyan king. Soon, a son, Rahula was born to them. At the age of twenty-nine, Siddartha went out to see the city of his father. He beheld what the Buddhist books call the "four signs," – witnesses to the impermanence of the world. He saw an old man, a diseased man, a dead man, and a monk. And there entered into his heart a vision of *dukkha*, the world-sorrow. "What is the way out of the world-sorrow?" he asked himself, repeatedly.

It was a dark hour of the night. Gautama thought, "I must leave this palace and go out into the darkness of the Great Unknown, and in that darkness, find the Light of my life." Gautama would fain caress at his son before leaving the palace. But, he was afraid to awaken Yashodhara. Both the son and the mother were fast asleep. He gazed at both. Tears touched his eyes: he turned away, and left in silence.

He goes out upon his quest. He renounces the palace to go in search of a cure for the cruelties and stupidities of life.

It is indeed, a moving story, Gautama's quest that ends in illumination and attainment of *nirvana*. On reaching the forest of meditation, he gives away his fine clothes to his charioteer, Channa, saying, "These fine Banaras silks do not befit a *sramana*!" Gautama, the prince, becomes a *fakir*. He enters the forest.

For six years, did Gautama practise intense asceticism. For several days in succession, he ate only one grain of rice. His strong, athletic body was reduced to a bag of bones. But it served no purpose! The Buddha then scattered a handful of grass on the ground beneath the Bodhi tree and formed a seat for himself. "I care not if my skin and nerves and bones decay!" he thought. "I care not if my life-blood dries, I shall not give up until I attain to enlightenment."

What divine will-power in these words! And what may not a man achieve if he would wake up his will-power!

He beheld a vision of some dancing girls, singing joyfully. Buddha listened to their song. It seemed that the song contained a message for him: it acted as a spiritual stimulant to him. It infused in him new strength, courage. The words were:

> Tune the *sitar* neither low nor high,
> The string overstretched breaks and the music dies.
> The string overslack is dumb and music dies.

He thought to himself, "I too, have tortured my body to starvation. I have taken to extremes. Let me follow the middle path."

Even as he made this resolve, a beautiful girl named Sujata, appeared before him, carrying a golden bowl filled with sweetened milk and rice, which was meant to be an offering to the river.

When she saw the Buddha, she felt that she beheld the Lord of the river incarnate. In reverence and devotion, she offered the bowl at his feet.

Buddha accepted her offering. He drank the milk and threw the cup into the river. "If the cup reaches the other shore," he said to himself, "I shall receive enlightenment today."

And so it came to pass!

Born under a tree, the Buddha received illumination also, under a tree. To this day, we venerate this tree as the Bodhi Tree.

The Buddha's first impulse, on attaining illumination, was to withdraw from the world. But, the Compassionate One that he was, he saw that the world needed his ministration and his message. He was filled with pity for the people. And, filled with compassion, he went out among them to give his message.

The task was by no means easy! It was no path of roses that lay before him. In the early days of his mission, he met every form of abuse, opposition, and persecution. But he chose the way of love! He conquered by love.

His opponents called him a thief, because he had 'destroyed faith in animal sacrifices'! "Do not see even his face," they said of him. Once, he went hungry, as no one in a village was prepared to give him even a morsel of food as alms!

Sonadanda was a learned Brahmin. People advised this scholar not to see the Buddha, for it would affect his reputation adversely!

Sundari was a nun. The Buddha's opponents arranged for hired killers to murder her and throw her body in the woods near the Buddha's monastery.

"It is Gautama who perpetrated this heinous crime!" cried his opponents. Gautama was quiet, patient, and forgiving. One day, the hired assassins got drunk and, in their intoxicated condition, revealed the conspiracy. Thus, the real culprits were brought to book, and the Buddha's enemies were put to shame.

Cinca was a beautiful young woman. The Buddha's enemies bribed her to accuse the Master of having an illicit relationship with her. Misguided and misled by these men, she took up a wooden globe and made herself appear like a pregnant woman. Her false accusations made the Buddha's enemies revile him in public. The Buddha remained unaffected by the slander and malice. He was calm, silent and serene. However, this plan was also foiled by Divine Will. In the ninth month, the young woman appeared at the Buddha's evening *satsang*, to make a public accusation against the Buddha in the presence of the people. She accused the Master of having lived with her and demanded that *he* should provide her with a place for her approaching confinement.

The Buddha remained calm. In gentle words, he said to her, "Sister! Whether your words be true or not, nobody knows but you and I." At these words, the woman's wooden globe fell down in public! The people saw the truth, and they hooted her out and pursued her till she confessed the truth and begged for forgiveness.

Devadatta was a cousin and disciple of the Buddha; but that did not stop him from turning a traitor to the Master. Devadatta was jealous of the Buddha's growing fame and the eminence in which people held him. He wished to be the leader of the Sangha. He spread malicious slanders against the Buddha and even hired men to murder the Master. These desperadoes went to kill the Buddha – but, they remained to revere him! In his sacred presence their hearts were conquered, and they were converted. They fell at the Master's feet: they confessed their sin: they repented and asked him to accept them as his disciples.

The Buddha's Way was ever the Way of quenching sorrow. On one occasion, he gave his teaching in a few significant words: "Quench the flames!" He pointed out that three "flames" threatened to destroy man:

(1) the flame of greed,

(2) the flame of the "ego", the "I", and

(3) the flame of hate.

"Quench the flames," he urged people, again and yet again.

Now kings left their kingdoms and sought to follow him. Buddha was the unique Master in history whose father, son and wife were initiated into the order by himself!

The story of this marvellous man, who wrought his miracles of mercy passed from the Caucasian language to the Greek and thence to Latin as the "Story of Barlaam and Jesophat." The teaching of the Buddha has appeared in translations into Tibetan, Chinese and Turkish languages and in several dialects in India. In a Museum in Russia lies, still unpublished, the text of many of the "Sayings and Parables and Dialogues" of the Buddha.

The Buddha lived to the age of eighty years. Forty-five of these years he spent in teaching. In fact, he preached to the very last day of his earth-life. He preached and he healed the lame, the deaf and the blind.

The Buddha abjured all violence.

There is one story, which I would like to narrate to you: it is a story which has moved me profoundly. It is, indeed, a beautiful illustration of the Buddha's compassion for animals.

The incident came to pass at Rajgir, where the Buddha was taking a walk, one day. He was captivated by the beauty of the natural scenery around him. He saw birds and animals being sheltered by the tall trees and marvelled at the inherent kindness of nature, as against man's cruelty to defenseless creatures.

Just then, a flock of goats and sheep passed by him. The Buddha saw that the herdsman had great difficulty in driving the animals forward.

"What is the matter?" the Buddha enquired of him.

The herdsman pointed out to the Master, a lame lamb in the herd. This little creature was unable to keep pace with the others, and thus the entire herd had to slow down because of him.

The very soul of affection, the Buddha took the limping lamb on his shoulder, and began to walk with the herdsman and his flock.

"Pray tell me," he said to the herdsman, "Why are you driving the herd in the heat of the noonday sun?"

The herdsman replied that he had been commanded to give the King one hundred goats and sheep for sacrifice in a *yagna* which was to be performed that evening.

The Buddha said to him, "I too, shall go to this *yagna* with you!"

Soon thereafter, they reached the city – the radiant Master, with the lamb on his shoulder, walking side by side with the herdsman. Their path lay through a crowded marketplace; and the buyers and sellers gazed in awe and reverence at the graceful, gentle countenance of the Master, who walked among them, so peacefully, so quietly. Who was this angel of compassion, they wondered. The Master moved on. And the people simply could not take their eyes off him! They hardly knew him; only a few had even heard of him. "Who is this holy man?" they wondered.

And so the Buddha reached the place where the *yagna* was being performed.

All preparations had been made for the animal sacrifice. The Executioner was about to strike the sword against the first lamb marked for the sacrifice, when the Buddha's voice rang out, gently and firmly. "Great King! Let not the man strike! Take my life as a sacrifice, O King, and spare the lamb!"

The words startled the King, transforming his life and heart instantly. Humbly, he requested Gautama to speak to the people. And the Buddha uttered just a few words on the occasion:

"O man! You can take away a life easily but, remember, none of you can give life!

So have mercy, have compassion!

And, never forget, that compassion makes the world noble and beautiful.

Remember, too, that all living beings are linked together in *maitri*.

Therefore, resolve that you will live on blood-less diet.

For verily, in gentleness is the crown of life!"

The next day, the King promulgated a decree: *no one* shall henceforth kill for sacrifice or for private pleasure. For life is one: and the crown of life is mercy or compassion.

"Hold fast," said the Buddha, "to the lamp of *dharma*." And is not *maitri*, friendliness with all, the lamp of *dharma?* The Buddha showed people the way of peace, of loving compassion.

There is yet another memorable incident from his life, which I would like to relate to you.

Two kings belonging to two different realms, with their ranged armies, stood on the banks of the river, Rohini. The armies were there, to fight. But one hundred and sixty thousand women were there, too: they were weeping for their children, their husbands, their brothers and fathers, their near and dear ones. For war means slaughter! War means death and destruction!

What was the quarrel between the two kings? What was the battle being fought over? Each Kingdom was claiming its right over the *waters* of the river Rohini.

The Buddha had a nobler conception of kingship. The word for *king* in Pali is *khattriya* and the word means "protector", guardian". A true king is enjoined to be a "protector", a "guardian" of his people. How could he then indulge in war, which means the slaughter of thousands of sons and husbands and brothers and fathers?

The Buddha sees the two armies ranged, one against the other, on the banks of the Rohini, prepared to fight over water. He stands between the kings of the two armies.

"Tell me, O Kings," says the Buddha. "How much, do you think, is water worth?"

Each king says, "O Blessed One! You know and we know, water is worth very little!"

"How much," asks Buddha, "is this earth worth?"

And each king says, "O Blessed One! The earth is of great worth!"

"And how much," asks the Buddha, "are the kings worth?"

"Great is their worth," answers each king.

"And how much are your queens worth?" asks the Blessed One.

"The queens," said each, "are worth a great deal: I love my queen dearly!"

"And how much worth are the lives of your soldiers who are here to fight and slay one another?" asks the Buddha.

And each king says, "Precious to me is the life of every one of my soldiers: precious is their life-blood!"

"O ye wise Kings!" says the Buddha, "Why then are you out to destroy each other? Your queens are so dear to you, as are your people, and your soldiers. And yet, for the sake of a little water, you are prepared to risk their lives! Is not Peace better than letting flow a river of blood?"

There is, in the presence of the Buddha, a divine love which heals and illuminates.

And as the kings listen to the Blessed One, their weapons fall to the ground: they are silent, lost in speechless wonder.

There are lifelike paintings in some of the ancient *viharas*, depicting the two kings gazing at the divine beauty of the Buddha's countenance. How eager they seem to listen to the Lord!

And knowing their aspiration, the Master speaks to them:

"And in this world of strife and hate
With hearts filled with love we live!
And love alone for hate we give:
The world for Peace and Love doth wait."

How I wish the nations today would heed the Wisdom of the Buddha! Alas, we live in a war-torn world. When will we bear witness to the teachings of the Buddha, the Preacher of Great Peace and Love?

Let us bow our heads in reverence to the Lord of Peace, Compassion and *Maitri*.

Buddham sharanam gachhami
Sangam sharanam gachhami
Dhammam sharanam gachhami!

Sayings of Gautama Buddha

"O *bhikkhus!*
Wander through the land
With the message of healing
And the message of light.
And in the midst of darkness
Kindle ye the light that heals!
Thus, go ye forth to places near and places far!
And, filled with compassion,
Bring happiness to multitudes,
Bring new life to all!"

* * * * *

"This triple truth
Teach ye to all:
The generous heart,
The kindly speech,
The life of compassion and service—
These be the things
That make Humanity new!"

* * * * *

"May every living thing,
Weak or strong, tall or short,
Dwelling near or far away,
Born or yet in womb unborn,
May everything on earth
Breathing out the breath of life,
Be happy, full of bliss!"

* * * * *

"Brethren!
If, indeed, the robbers cross you on the way,
And with a two-handed saw
Carve you in pieces, limb by limb,
And you harbour for them hatred in your hearts,
Know, then, you are not worthy of me,
Nor of the message I come to give!"

Book by Gautama Buddha

- *Dhammapada*

Some Books on Gautama Buddha

- *Becoming Buddha: The Story of Siddhartha* – by Whitney Stewart, Tenzin Gyatso (HH Dalai Lama), and Sally Rippin
- *Buddha: A Story of Enlightenment* – by Deepak Chopra
- *Prince Siddhartha: The Story of Buddha* – by Jonathan Landaw
- *Treasures of the Buddha: The Glories of Sacred Asia* – by Tom Lowenstein
- *Buddha Stories* – by Demi
- *The Heart of the Buddha* (Dharma Ocean Series, 1) – by Chogyam Trungpa
- *The Dhammapada: The Essential Teachings of the Buddha (Sacred Wisdom)* – by Watkins
- *The Buddha: The Story of an Awakened Life* – by David Kherdian
- *The Prince Who Ran Away: The Story Of Gautama Buddha* – by Anne Rockwell and Fahimeh Amiri

Sant Tulsidas

Sant Tulsidas is one of the great singer-poet-saints of India. His divinely inspired songs and *shlokas* are recited by thousands of Hindus, both rich and poor, in towns, cities and villages across India. The grace of Sri Rama transformed Tulsidas's life and opened the fount of his inspiration. Therefore, it has been said, his songs will live as long as the rivers run and the sun shines in the heaven above!

Sant Tulsidas

When we think of Sant Tulsidas, we are reminded of Sri Rama. Sant Tulsidas was the author of the most popular and well-known version of the great epic which the centuries have revered as *Srimad Ramayana*. We refer to his composition as the *Ram Charita Manas*. Gandhiji regarded the *Ram Charita Manas* as the greatest book among all the spiritual literature of the world. Different versions of the *Ramayana* have been written. The first *Ramayana* was composed by Maharishi Valmiki. It was written in Sanskrit. We also have the *Anand Ramayana*, the *Uttar Ramayana*, the *Surya Ramayana* and the *Rangrat Ramayana*. But *Rama Charita Manas* is the most popular among the people of India.

The meaning of the word *Manas* is 'Mansarovar'. Sant Tulsidas felt that this great *shastra*, this great scripture, is a *sarovar* – a lake, from which we can obtain the ripples of Rama's *Charitra* or character: this is the lake which is filled with the waters of the character of Sri Rama.

Let us reflect upon the life of Sant Tulsidas. Goswami Tulsidas was born in a small village of Rajapur in 1554. His father's name was Atmaram Dubey and mother's name was Tulsi. Tulsidevi was a pious lady. His father was a renowned *pandit* or scholar. He was the assistant to the head of the village, and so was referred to as Raj Guru. It is said that child Tulsidas did not cry at the time of his birth, but instead repeated the word, 'Ram, Ram, Ram, Ram, Ram.'

Dear friends, have you ever seen or heard of such a child? A child who did not cry at the time of his birth, a child who instead uttered the words, 'Ram, Ram, Ram'? It is also said that his appearance was like that of a five year old child, and that he had all his 32 teeth! The father was frightened. He said to himself, "Who is this abnormal child born in my house?" He called for scholars, astrologers and priests and asked them to cast the horoscope. "We have never seen such a baby!" they exclaimed. "It will take us three days to observe him and give you the result of our studies."

After three days, they all arrived at a common view: the child was a bad omen; if he continued to stay in the house, he would bring bad fortune and the rest of the family members would suffer. They suggested that the father should abandon the child. Coincidentally, the mother fell ill around that time. On the fourth day, she became worried about her child. She therefore called for her maid servant, Muniya, and requested her to take away the child. "Take away all my ornaments, all my wealth but pray look after my little child," she pleaded with Muniya. "My life has almost come to an end. You must take my son with you and take good care of him. After my death, I don't know how my husband will treat this poor infant." Muniya took the child and left for her village.

As fate would have it, Tulsidevi passed away the very next day. Atmaram Dubey, the father, thought to himself, "I must not keep this child in my house, I must get rid of him." But the child was nowhere to be found! For her part, the maid servant took good care of the child. She named the child Ram Bola, because as soon as he was born, he had uttered the word 'Ram.' When Ram Bola was five years and five months old Muniya passed away. Atmaram Dubey, the father, was sent a message that the maid servant who took care of his child had also passed away. They asked him to come and take his son. Dubey refused to do so.

Ram Bola had no one to take care of him. He started roaming aimlessly on the streets. The people had a firm belief that the child brought ill luck wherever he went.

When he went begging, no one would even give him alms.

His sufferings soon came to an end when a saint visited their village. His name was Sant Nar Haridas. Nar Haridas was a true devotee of God. He took great care of Ram Bola.

The saint gave Ram Bola a lot of love and took him to Ayodhya. When the child turned seven, he was initiated with the sacred thread. To the astonishment of all, he started chanting the *Gayatri Mantra*.

Nobody had taught the child the *Gayatri Mantra*. People were amazed. The child regarded Sant Nar Haridas as his Guru. Nar Haridas bestowed on him the 'Rama Naam' *mantra*, and Ram Bola started reciting the *mantra*. Nar Haridas then took Ram Bola to a holy place called Uttarkhet, which is situated near Ayodhya. There he related to him the thrilling story of Sri Rama.

Ram Bola stayed with the Guru for seven years. Nar Haridas decided to leave for a pilgrimage and asked Ram Bola to accompany him. Both left for Kashi, where they met another saint named Sant Shreshtnathan. Sant Shreshtnathan kept gazing at Ram Bola. "You are so lucky to have this child," he exclaimed. "Can you leave him with me? I will teach him Sanskrit, and educate him. He is not an ordinary child. He has hidden powers, which, when revealed, will benefit mankind."

Nar Haridas had taken care of Ram Bola for seven years. He had loved Ram Bola as a father would love his son. But as he was a saint, he was not attached to anything or anyone. He immediately agreed to leave the child with Sant Shreshtnathan and continued on his pilgrimage.

The saint demonstrated a great truth by his detachment. Our children are not ours, our family members are not ours, but as long as they are with us, we should fulfill our duties towards them. We should love them and provide for their needs.

Ram Bola received knowledge of the scriptures from Sant Shreshtnathan for 15 years. At the end of that period, Sant Shreshtnathan passed away. Ram Bola returned to his home town, and decided to settle in the village. The unhappy omens of his unfortunate childhood were forgotten, and the villagers welcomed the young scholar.

Back in his village, Ram Bola was accepted as one among his people.

Every evening, Ram Bola narrated the *Rama Katha* to the villagers. Many of them gathered in his hut to listen to him. His fame spread far and wide. People from far away places came to the village to listen to him. One day, a priest, who lived on the other side of the Jamuna River, came to Rajapur. He was accompanied by his wife and other family members. His name was Deena Bandhu. He heard the *Rama Katha* of Sant Tulsidas. He was awe struck. He just kept gazing at Tulsidas. "He is a unique saint. His language is so simple, yet so profound," he exclaimed. He returned to his village, but after three months came back to Rajapur. "I have had a dream in which

Parvati Devi has asked me to get my daughter Ratnawali married to you," he implored Tulsidas.

"I don't want to get trapped in these relationships," Tulsidas replied. "I want to serve God all my life!"

"This is Parvati Devi's wish." Deena Bandhu insisted. "Will you not obey her? If you don't marry my daughter," he added, "I will go on a fast until death."

He sat outside Sant Tulsidas's hut and said that he would not move till Tulsidas consented.

Now, Ratnawali was a very beautiful girl. Sant Tulsidas married her. He was simply enchanted by her beauty, and very attracted to her. Ratnawali was everything in his life. He would hover around her all day. He was truly besotted, infatuated by her beauty.

Soon, a child was born to them. Generally after a child is born, the parents get attached to the baby, but Sant Tulsidas started loving his wife all the more. He would not leave her company even for a single moment. Ratnawali's parents would request her to come home but Sant Tulsidas would not allow her to go to them, even for a day!

One day when Sant Tulsidas left his house for some work, Ratnawali's brother arrived with a message. "Mother and father are anxious to meet you. They want to see their grandson. Since Tulsidas is away, let me take you." Ratnawali was also anxious to meet her parents. She got ready and they left.

After some time Tulsidas returned home. He was anguished when he did not find Ratnawali at home. She was the light of his life! She was everything to him! He looked all around for her. Not finding her anywhere, he cried out, "Ratnawali, Ratnawali, where are you?" He stood on the road and asked passers-by if they had seen Ratnawali. The people made fun of him. But Tulsidas was disconsolate with grief. He continued to call out, "Ratnawali! Ratnawali!" A passer-by looked at him and smiled. Seeing his smile, Tulsidas thought that this man knew something about Ratnawali's whereabouts. "Her brother had come to take her home and she left with him. Ratnawali is very happy there," exclaimed the stranger.

Tulsidas immediately decided to leave for Ratnawali's village. It was late in the evening. He had to cross a forest where ferocious animals lived. But Tulsidas was infatuated and in this stage nothing could stop him. He only wanted to meet Ratnawali. He crossed the forest and reached Ratnawali's village.

He reached Ratnawali's house well past midnight. The door of the home was locked. He noticed a rope hanging from the roof. He used the rope to climb up and entered Ratnawali's room. Ratnawali was sleeping. He woke her up, and she was shocked to see him there. "How did you reach here at this time of the night?" she inquired. "How did you cross the forest? How did you manage to get here upstairs to my room?"

Tulsidas replied, "There was a rope hanging outside and I used it to get to your room." Ratnawali came out to check the rope but found that what Tulsidas thought to be a rope, was, in reality, a snake hanging on the wall. In desperation she said to him, "Husband! You are so attached to my physical form. If you could offer even half of this love to Sri Rama, you would reach *swarga loka*."

Ratnawali had just uttered these words, and as if by lightning, they struck his consciousness deeply and Sant Tulsidas, who was already a devotee of Sri Rama, was transformed in that one instant!

God's grace works in mysterious ways. Some saints undergo *tapasya* and severe austerities for years. Tulsidas's life changed in one miraculous moment. He immediately left his wife and started chanting the holy Name of Sri Rama unceasingly. His life was now changed completely.

Tulsidas proceeded to Prayag. He left for a pilgrimage to various other places and finally settled in Banaras. He passed through many experiences and was inspired to write the *Ramayana*. To his astonishment he found that the *slokas* which he wrote in Sanskrit, would simply disappear as soon as he wrote them! He then had a vision of Lord Siva and Parvati who directed him to write the *Ramayana* in the vernacular — the language of the people, *Hindi*, so that it could be accessible to the masses, and easily understood by them.

Tulsidas now started to write the *Ramayana* in Hindi. It took him seven months and twenty-six days to complete the work.

The *pandits* of Banaras were jealous of him. They employed different people and made plots to steal his work. But at every step, Lord Rama protected him.

The *pandits* were angry with Tulsidas because he had made the great epic available to the common people in their own mother tongue, Hindi. But Tulsidas's intention was not to dishonour the Sanskrit language – he only wanted the poorest in the land to take a sip of the immortal nectar of Lord Rama's life – to take a dip in the sacred lake of His Name.

It is said that when Tulsidas gave public recitals of his Ramayana, Lord Hanuman himself came to listen to the beautiful songs, and sat among the audience in the form of an old brahmin.

When Tulsidas went to Brindavan, he found devotees of Sri Rama and Sri Krishna quarrelling with each other. When the poet-saint came to have *darshana* at Brindavan, Sri Krishna's statue was miraculously turned into a statue of Sri Rama, with bow and arrow in hand! Thus did Tulsidas prove that God was but One, while his *avatars* are many.

Sant Tulsidas left his physical body on the third day of Krishna Tritya in 1588 AD on the banks of the sacred River Ganga.

Centuries unborn will salute him for his great contribution to the literature, religion, culture and faith of this great land!

Sayings of Sant Tulsidas

"The lowliest of the low is blessed,
If he worship the Lord,
By day and night.
O ye of the highest caste,
What gain ye in life,
If ye sing not the Holy Name?"
"I have seen the rich and the great
Of the nations of the Earth.
Not one of them, I say,
Is equal unto him
Who is a *bhakta*,
A servant of the Beloved,
And who each night and day
With every breath doth say:
'Holy, holy is Thy Name!'"
"From place to place
He wandereth still,
To give to men the knowledge
That illumines and purifies!
Blessed, indeed, is the land
Where dwell such holy ones.
Love is the law of their life:
Helpers are they – and healers.
Their senses are subdued,
Their thoughts do dwell
On none but the Lord.
To the One are they devoted, ever true!
And in their hearts they know
The world is but a dream.
And as the cuckoo
Doth in rainy season long
For a drop of rain,
So long they for the Lord!"

Some Works by Sant Tulsidas

- Rama Charita Mânasa
- Hanuman Chalisa
- Vinaya Patrika
- Dohavali
- Kabitta Ramayan or Kavitavali
- Gitavali
- Baravai Ramayana
- Janaki Mangal
- Ramalala Nahachhu
- Ramajna Prashna
- Parvati Mangal
- Krishna Gitavali
- Hanuman Bahuka
- Sankata Mochana
- Vairagya Sandipini

Some Books on Sant Tulsidas

- *Lives of Saints* – Swami Sivananda
- *Tulsidas* – by Devendra Singh
- *The Ramayan of Tulsidas Or the Bible of Northern India* – by J. M. Macfie
- *A Short Biography of Goswami Tulsidas* – by Bibhor Kumar Lahiri
- *Stories of Indian Saints* – by Mahipati
- *The Philosophy of Tulsidas* – by Ramdat Bharadwaj
- *The Oracle of Rama*: An Adaptation of *Rama Ajna Prashna* of Goswami Tulsidas – by David Frawley
- *The Life of a Text*: Performing the *Ramcharitmanas* of Tulsidas – by Philip Lutgendorf
- *Love and Truth in the Ramayana of Tulsidas* – by Anantanand Rambachan
- *Tulsidas* (Mystic Saints of India) – by B.K. Chaturvedi and Tulasidasa

Guru Nanak

Guru Nanak was a symbol of the Universal Man. At a time when India was weakened by religious bigotry and mutual hatred, Guru Nanak was bold enough to declare that there is no Hindu and no Mussalman; and that all of us are children of the One Heavenly Father. The emphasis in his message was not on rites and rituals, creeds and ceremonies, but on love of God and loving service of fellow-men. Guru Nanak's message of brotherhood and peace, of love and harmony can heal the wounds with which India's soul lies wounded today.

Guru Nanak

Guru Nanak was one of the most radiant stars in the firmament of India's spiritual leaders. His face was so luminous that people saw him and they bowed down to him of their own accord. On this dark planet he appeared as a heavenly light. And this light continues to shine even today in millions of hearts. It is the light of love.

Guru Nanak gave his love to all – to Hindus and Muslims, Indians and Arabs, Persians and Afghans. In them all he saw the one glory of Divine Humanity.

He was a prophet of harmony. I salute him as a master of a million hearts – one of the greatest spiritual luminaries in Indian history, in the history of humanity.

Guru Nanak was born on April 15, 1469, at Talwandi, a village about forty miles to the south-west of Lahore (now in Pakistan). His mother's name was Tripta: full of devotion was she and full of tender love for her son Nanak. His father, Mehta Kalu, was a *pateri* or accountant to the Muslim landlord of the village, Rai Bular, by name.

Nanak was a very intelligent child. He was sent to a school where he learnt the alphabet in no time.

Child Nanak would ask his teacher, "Does this knowledge have any significance without love?"

How true it is that knowledge without love is empty and hollow! Knowledge without love does not have any significance.

"Speak to me," said Nanak, "about the Creator and His creation. For all learning is in vain without a knowledge of Him. And to know Him, to realise Him, we need to love Him."

Child Nanak's words left his teacher astonished! The teacher met the father and said, "Your son is far wiser than I! I am not capable of teaching him, for he is a great sage."

However, child Nanak's father was not really happy with his son. He was unable to appreciate the child's wisdom and perception. All that the father wanted was that the son should acquire fame and worldly wealth. So his constant advice to his son was to set up a business of his own. But the son was lost in a world of his own, even as his eyes overflowed with intense love for the Almighty!

One day, child Nanak was gifted a gold ring. As we know, children are fascinated by glittering and precious things like gold, but this was not so in child Nanak's case. The gold ring was but as brass to the child.

He put on the gold ring and went out of his house. At that time, a *sanyasi*, a hermit, met him. The hermit was very hungry; he said that he had been starved of food for some days. On hearing this, child Nanak, without hesitation, offered his gold ring to the hermit and asked him to sell the ring and get some food. He also asked the *sanyasi* to chant the Name of the Lord, with love and devotion.

Nanak was never enamoured by material possessions – by gold or silver. He was absorbed in the thought and Name of the Lord.

The father did his best to interest his son in worldly matters. He asked Nanak to take the cows to the grazing ground. Nanak let the cows graze as they pleased while he sat down to meditate!

The father, then, put him in charge of a shop, but the son distributed the groceries among the *Sadhus* and the poor and the needy.

The father was at a loss to understand his son! In despair, he said to Nanak, "My son, it looks as if you are an utter failure in life! Wouldn't you like to be someone in society? You must do something or the other to earn wealth. Why don't you take to farming? Be a farmer and plough the fields." And Nanak said to his father: "Father, I am ploughing the fields of life. I am sowing in my life, the seeds of the Name Divine!"

No matter how hard the father tried, he could not bring his son down to earth. Indeed, on one occasion he said, "It would be easier to catch hold of the rays of the rising sun!"

One day, Kalu gave his son twenty rupees and sent him to a nearby market to strike a profitable bargain. On the way Nanak found a group of *sanyasins* who looked starved. Nanak purchased food and fed the *sanyasins* to their satisfaction. They felt happy and blessed Nanak profusely.

When his father asked him what he had done with the money, Nanak replied, "I struck the most profitable bargain! I fed the poor ascetics who were starved to death. What better bargain than this, father?"

At the age of nineteen Nanak was married to Sulakhni, for the family felt that marriage and family life would, perhaps, change him. Nanak had two sons, Sri Chand and Lakhmi Chand.

If there was one member of the family who understood and had regard for Nanak, it was his sister, Nanaki. She was married to Jairam, who was employed with the Nawab of Sultanpur. Jairam arranged for Nanak to be appointed as the *Modi* in charge of the Imperial Stores. It is believed that Nanak was in the service of the Nawab for 10 years. He worked so well that everyone was pleased with him and exclaimed: "What a man! What a man!"

One day people saw Guru Nanak going for a dip in the river. No one saw him come out of the river. He went missing for three whole days. At the end of the third day, Nanak appeared. His eyes glowed with a strange light. He had had a vision. In the vision he heard a voice tell him: "Nanak, I am with Thee. Repeat My Name and ask others to repeat My Name; mingle with men and show them the way!"

Now his life's mission became clear to Nanak. He prepared to go forth among the people, to sing to them the Name of God. He undertook several long journeys, mostly on foot, to propagate the message of unity, harmony and love. He travelled far and wide; he went to Mecca, Baghdad, Afghanistan, Ceylon, Tibet; he travelled all over India and Kashmir. Wherever he went, he awakened the souls of the people. He revealed to prince and peasant, to Hindus and Muslims, to the educated and illiterate, the way to reach God.

Let me narrate to you, just *one* of the many inspiring events from the life of this great Guru.

During his travels, Guru Nanak, accompanied by his friend and follower, Mardana, arrived at Saidpur. They knocked on the door of a poor carpenter, called Laloo. Laloo was busy with his carpentry. Guru Nanak knocked again and called, "What are you doing, Laloo?"

"Mending wooden pegs," Laloo replied, continuing his work.

"Has life no better purpose?" the Guru asked in a penetrating voice. "Come to me, and I shall show you how to mend yourself!"

Laloo left his tools and came and fell at the Guru's feet. He offered himself wholly to him. Guru Nanak stayed with him for sometime.

The news that a man of God was staying at the house of a low caste carpenter, spread like wild fire in Saidpur. The most powerful man in Saidpur, Malik Bhago, was infuriated. He was given to oppressing the poor and the lowly. A sacrificial feast was being organised by him and he sent an invitation to Guru Nanak to attend it. The Guru declined the invitation.

A special representative was sent to request the Guru, once again, to attend the feast. Guru Nanak came to the sacrificial feast, but refused to partake of any food. "How can you refuse my food, and accept the food of a low caste carpenter?" Malik Bhago asked in anger.

"I recognise no caste or creed," replied the Guru calmly. "I cannot partake of food obtained by oppressing the poor." And he added, "O Malik, while Laloo's dry crumbs of bread contain milk, your dainty dishes contain the blood of the oppressed! How then can I eat the food you offer me?"

Bhago realised his mistake and immediately fell at the feet of Guru Nanak. The Guru looked on him with mercy and said to him, "Distribute your wealth among the oppressed and live a new life!"

His travels took the Guru to many parts of the land. His disciple, Mardana, always accompanied him. Once in the course of their travel, dacoits from the Chambal valley happened to cross their path. These bandits were professional kidnappers who sold captive travellers as slaves. One of the bandits caught sight of the luminous face of Guru Nanak. He was fascinated by the Guru and thought to himself that if this man were sold, he would be able to procure an exorbitant price for him.

The bandit thought of tricking Guru Nanak! But who could deceive a man who was as holy as he was wise? The Guru let the bandit play his trick. The bandit kidnapped Guru Nanak and took him away. Mardana was left behind. Before leaving, Guru Nanak told Mardana, "I am going on a trip and will return as soon as I can. In the meantime, you must wait here." He also told him about several verdant woods nearby, from where he could get fruits to satisfy his hunger. Assuring Mardana that he would return soon, Guru Nanak left on his long journey with the bandit.

He was brought to the bandit's house in Chambal. On seeing Guru Nanak, the bandit's wife was enthralled by the glow on his face and wished to adopt him as her son, for she did not have a child of her own. To this the bandit replied, "If I sell him in a market, I will earn a large sum of money. Why should I lose such an enormous amount of money by adopting this handsome, charming lad as a son? I will bring another young lad for you, whom you can adopt as a son. In the meantime, you can get this young man to do some work for you."

Some days passed and suddenly there was a severe famine in the town. The weather became stormy and dark clouds appeared in the skies, though there was no rain. The people were worried, as it was difficult to survive without water and food. They lived in the constant shadow of death. The bandit's wife turned to Guru Nanak for moral support. She felt that the charming young man staying at her home, was an honest man, a good human being. "The Divine Light of the Almighty shines in his eyes," she thought. "His way of life is the way of the Spirit. He wakes up very early in morning, at three or four o'clock and does *kirtan*, in his melodious and soulful voice!" Listening to his *kirtan*, her mind seemed to go in a trance, making her feel at peace even though she was unable to understand his language. Further, she reflected, "I think this young man can free us from this life-threatening situation by showing us a way out." Accordingly, she spoke to her husband, the bandit, and his friends. They approached Guru Nanak and requested him to help them out of the calamity that had befallen them.

Guru Nanak said to them, "My friends, all that is happening to you, is the result of your *karma*, a reaction to your cruel and evil acts. You kidnap people, innocent human beings and make them your slaves. You have caused grief to poor, innocent people. These inhuman acts of yours, are the cause of the famine which afflicts you."

Guru Nanak's words alarmed everyone. They began to question themselves, "Is there anything we can do to rectify the situation now? Shall we die?"

Guru Nanak said to them, "God is just – and He is also merciful. If you repent and ask God for God's forgiveness and mercy, He will pardon your sins. But on one condition – that you will sin no more and distribute your ill-gotten wealth in service of the poor and lowly!"

The dacoits begged Guru Nanak to give them guidance. The great Guru replied, "The first thing you must do is to free your slaves, and spend your ill-begotten wealth in service of the poor and needy. After you do this, we will beg God for forgiveness and pray for His mercy. I am sure the All Merciful One will have mercy on us."

The bandits conferred among themselves and did what they were asked to do. Then they joined Guru Nanak in *kirtan*. Suddenly, they found that the weather had changed and the clouds started pouring rain on the dry earth. The days of famine were over: the rivers, lakes and wells were filled with water. And the people rejoiced.

The life of Guru Nanak is filled with many such incidents. For twenty-five years the great Guru moved from place to place, spreading solace and comfort wherever he went and asking the people to sing the Holy Name, to rejoice in all conditions and circumstances of life and to render the service of love to the poor and lonely, the unwanted and the unloved.

Towards the closing period of his life, he settled down at Kartarpur. Everyday, in the early hour of the dawn, *satsang* was held which was attended by a number of aspiring souls.

According to some scholars, on Monday, September 22, 1539, Guru Nanak's earthly pilgrimage came to a close. Guru Nanak was a farmer who planted seeds of faith and devotion in many aspiring hearts – the seeds of a new faith, a new vision, a new life. He founded no sect, for he revered all religions. In all he beheld the Light of God.

I have often recalled to myself the touching words of Gurudev Sadhu Vaswani. In his inspiring book on Guru Nanak, he writes: "As I have recalled incident after incident of his life, I have sometimes said to myself: "O, that I had the privilege his first disciples had, of hearing his wondrous words and seeing the sacred beauty of His Lotus Face and kissing his Lotus Feet! Then a nobler thought came to me and I say to myself: Alas! I forget that he has passed into the Unseen only to come nearer to us in Spirit. He has gone away in order to enter into us, into the life of India, the life of the world. Is he not still our Leader and our Light?"

Homage to him!

Sayings of Guru Nanak

"Let no man in the world live in delusion. Without a Guru none can cross over to the other shore."

* * * * *

"The word is the Guru, The Guru is the word. For all nectar is enshrined in the word. Blessed is the word which reveals the Lord's Name. But more is the one who knows by the Guru's grace."

* * * * *

"God is one, but He has innumerable forms. He is the Creator of all, and He Himself takes the human form."

* * * * *

"One cannot comprehend Him through reason, even if one reasoned for ages."

* * * * *

"The Lord can never be established nor created; the Formless One is limitlessly complete in Himself."

* * * * *

"Even Kings and emperors with heaps of wealth and vast dominion cannot compare with an ant filled with the love of God."

* * * * *

"As fragrance abides in the flower,
As reflection is within the mirror,
So does your Lord abide within you,
Why search for Him without?"

* * * * *

"I am not the born; how can there be either birth or death for me?"

* * * * *

"The Lord God, the Giver of peace, has granted His Grace, I am rid of pain, sin and disease."

* * * * *

"He who shows the real home in this body is the Guru. He makes the five-sounded word reverberate in man."

Some Books on Guru Nanak

- *Guru Nanak* – by Sadhu T. L. Vaswani
- *The First Sikh Spiritual Master*: Timeless Wisdom from the Life and Techniques of Guru Nanak – by Harish Dhillon
- *Guru for the Aquarian Age*: The Life and Teachings of Guru Nanak – by Steve Gilbar and Parmatma Singh Khalsa
- *Illustrated Stories from the Life of Guru Nanak Dev Ji* – by Ajit Singh Aulukh
- *Guru Nanak: His Life & Teachings* – by Roopinder Singh
- *Life Story of Guru Nanak* – by Surinder Singh Johar
- *The Divine Master; Life and Teachings of Guru Nanak Dev* – by Sewaram Singh
- *Guru Nanak and Sikhism* (Great Religious Leaders) – by Rajinder Singh Panesar

Sri Ramakrishna Paramahansa

Sri Ramakrishna Paramahansa is without a parallel in the hagiology of the world, in that he actually practised the spiritual disciplines laid down by different religious traditions and declared that all led to the One God. He showed us through his life and teachings that though the paths are many, the Goal is One. In his life, God-realisation was beautifully blended with service of God-in-man. Every man, howsoever poor, was to him a living, moving shrine of God. Sri Ramakrishna's message of love, harmony and freedom can still rejuvenate the nations.

Sri Ramakrishna Paramahansa

Sri Ramakrishna Paramahansa was one of the noblest souls, one of the most profound beings that ever lived on earth. What can I say to you about him and his message? I am a child of silence – the silences of nature and the deeper silences of the soul. I have watched the silent moon, the silent stars. I have felt the silent power of the sun's rays. In silence I have listened to the singing of the birds. In silence I have watched the graceful movement of the river and listened to the voice of the murmuring brook which declares, 'Men may come and men may go but I go on for ever.' In silence I have felt the profound influence of the saints. In silence I have meditated upon the great mystery – the mystery of the ages, the mystery of the sages, the mystery of life. And Sri Ramakrishna Paramahansa was a lover of silence. He lived far away from the fret and fever of life. He lived far away from the maddening crowds of men. In a village, in a quiet corner, and then in a big temple, he lived. In a quiet corner in the temple of Dakshineshwar he lived, offering worship every day to Kali – the Divine Mother of the Universe. Every day, he gave the benedictions of his heart to so many who came for his *darshan* and for his blessings.

Sri Ramakrishna Paramahansa was born in a little village named Kamarpurkar in Bengal on February 18, 1836. His father and mother were God fearing and pious. Poor were they in the wealth of the world, but rich in the treasures of the heart. And though there were occasions when they did not have sufficient food for themselves, they did not hesitate in sharing what little they had with the poor and starving ones. From his childhood, Sri Ramakrishna who was called Gadhadar, was brought up in an atmosphere of poverty but also of contentment. He was endowed with an unusual mind and from his early days, his mind was inclined towards God. In other ways he was full of fun and frolic, love and laughter. He was sent to school but he did not take interest in school subjects, least of all in Mathematics. Arithmetic was the subject he simply could not learn. His teacher tried to pump knowledge into his head but Gadhadar was unresponsive until one day, in a mood of exasperation, the teacher sent word to his elder brother: "It were easier to teach the desk on which Gadhadar writes rather than to teach Gadhadar. Please do not send the boy to school any longer."

And when the elder brother spoke to Gadhadar of this, Gadhadar said to him, "Brother, of what use to me is this – a mere bread-and-butter earning education?" Even in those days when he was a child, Sri Ramakrishna had a high notion, a higher conception of education than most people hold. Later on, he would compare worldly minded intellectuals with kites and vultures which soared high up in the skies but whose eyes are all the time searching, searching for rotten pieces of flesh on the ground below. Likewise, Sri Ramakrishna observed, that the worldly intellectuals talk of high philosophy, high theology and high religion — but their minds are all the time fixed on *kanchan* and *kamini*, women and gold, on name and fame, on earthly power.

Gadhadar was fond of holy company. Whenever a *Sadhu* or a wandering *sanyasi* came to his village, Gadhadar would forget everything else. For hours, he would go and sit in the company of *sadhus* or wandering ascetics and listen to their *kathas* — their stories of the great ones who have blessed India age after age. Gadhadar was fond of holy company and he was fond of religious music; he was a lover of solitude and silence. Several hours every day, he would sit in a quiet corner, in a quiet nook underneath a tree, or on the riverbank, meditating in silence on the mystery of life; and even in those early days, he was blessed with spiritual visions.

As he grew in years, he grew in beauty. He grew in the power of solitude. When he was sixteen years old, he came to Calcutta and began to serve as a priest in the Dakshineshwar temple, where worship is offered unto Kali, the Divine Mother of the Universe. Gadhadar regarded Kali as his own mother; he called her his Divine Mother. The Divine Mother, to him, was not a mere idol, a mere statue. He would often say, "Even as I dwell within this body, so does the

Divine Mother dwell within this idol." And he would cry out again and again and still again, "O Mother mine, O Mother Divine! Reveal thyself to me! Reveal thyself to me!"

Gradually, the flood gates of his heart opened and the rituals and formalities of worship were discarded. His worship now consisted wholly of this cry of longing, this deep yearning of the soul. He would weep, he would shed tears as he cried out, "Mother! Mother! When will you reveal yourself to me? Hide not your beauteous face from your child." Then it was that he got his first vision of the Mother Divine. He felt uplifted. He felt as though he was swimming in an ocean of bliss. But this first experience was but a temporary experience. It wakened his appetite for more such visions. He wanted this temporary vision to be an abiding reality. And so, he continued to call out to the Divine Mother in deep longing, again and again.

This first experience he had received without any external help, without the help of any teacher. Now teachers began to come to him. Usually it is the disciple who moves out in quest of the teacher. In Ramakrishna's case it was the reverse. Teachers came to him one after another! Day after day, night after night, Ramakrishna spent in meditation and in spiritual disciplines. Food and sleep were forgotten. Outwardly he looked like a mad man. He was intoxicated, he was God intoxicated. His family began to feel anxious about him and they proposed marriage to bring him down to earth, to bring his mind down to the human plane.

And so, Ramakrishna was married. But it was a strange marriage! For Sri Ramakrishna always regarded women as so many forms of the Divine Mother. And his Divine consort, Sri Saradamani, was singularly free from all sex consciousness. Till the last she lived with him, nursing him, attending to his needs, serving him, being blessed by him, sharing his spiritual experiences.

The spiritual experiences of Sri Ramakrishna cover a wide range. He had a vision of the personal God and he realised his complete identity with the impersonal God – the spirit, the universal son! Sri Ramakrishna had a vision of Sri Rama, he had a vision of Sri Krishna, he had a vision of Jesus Christ.

One day Sri Ramakrishna expressed the desire to visit Kashi – and one of his rich admirers, Shri Mathura Babu, (who was the son-in-law of Rani Rashmani who built the Dakhshineshwar temple), agreed to make arrangements for the saint to visit Kashi. He said to Sri Ramakrishna, "Master, let me take you to Kashi." The two moved out on their journey. On the way they halted at a village. The village folk heard that a saint was in their midst. How they flocked together from near and far! They gathered together to have a *darshan* of the saint. "The blessed one has come," they said to each other in joy. They gazed and gazed and gazed at Sri Ramakrishna and in his face they beheld a beauty richer than flowers and more radiant then the stars. Sri Ramakrishna also looked at the villagers.

Their faces were pinched, their forms were emaciated. The poor villagers were ill fed, ill clothed!

Then he turned to Mathura Babu and said, "Mathura Babu, you are a Steward of the Mother. For, remember, the wealth that has been given you is a trust with you to be spent in the service of God and his suffering children. Mathura Babu, look at the village folk, they are poor, they are ill-fed, ill-clad. Kindly arrange to give them food and clothing and let each one have a piece of cloth." Mathura Babu did his calculations. The worldly man always calculates. And Mathura Babu thought to himself, to feed them will not cost so very much but to give a piece of cloth to every one of these villagers will cost a lot of money.

Mathura Babu hesitated. Sri Ramakrishna understood his mind. He did not speak a single word. This is the method of the saints. It is so unlike the method of the reformers. The reformers talk, they give lectures but the method of the saints is a quiet, gentle method. Quietly Sri Ramakrishna went and sat with the poor village folk. And after some time Mathura Babu said to him, "Master, it is time for us to resume our journey, we have to move on to Kashi." And Sri Ramakrishna said to him, "My child, my Kashi is here, my Kashi is at the feet of the poor. I do not want to proceed any further."

Yes, true it is that to the saint of God, Kashi is at the lotus feet of the poor. For the Beloved is where the broken ones are. My revered master, Sadhu Vaswani, used to say to us again and again, "Never forget this great truth, that the poor are the pictures of God. To serve them is to worship God." When you serve the poor, serve them in this spirit of worshipping God and you will be richly blessed!

Mathura Babu listened to these words, he felt ashamed of his conduct. Now he arranged for the feeding of the poor and sent an order to Calcutta for bales of cloth. When the bales of cloth arrived and when every one of those poor folk received a piece of cloth, Sri Ramakrishna felt free to move on.

Sri Ramakrishna was so like a child! As a child he lived among men, with the tender grace and beauty of a child of God. He addressed God as his mother, *"Ma! Ma! Ma!"* He would cry out again and again and go into *Samadhi*.

When two women of ill fame came to tempt him — he looked at them. He realised that they had come to him with an evil intention. He cried to God, *"Ma! Ma!"* He went into *Samadhi*.

On another occasion, some beautiful girls came to him, filled with the conceit of power and beauty which they thought the saint will not be able to resist. Once again he cried to God, *"Ma! Ma!"* and went into *Samadhi* and the Mother, as always, guarded him. When he came to normal consciousness the girls repented. They said to themselves, what a sin we have committed in having come to tempt this saint, this holy man of God. They fell at his feet, they asked for forgiveness, they became his disciples.

Sri Ramakrishna always lived as a child. As a child he talked to himself, to his body. He was fond of sweets known as *jelabi*. He used to call the *jelabi* as the 'Viceroy's carriage'. He said, there is always room for the viceroy's carriage. Every other food must make place for the *jelabi*. When the *jelabi* comes, all other foods must make way!

One day he visited Keshub Chandra Sen's residence and Keshub Chandra Sen sent for a plate full of *jelabis*. The *jelabis* were placed before Sri Ramakrishna. And Sri Ramakrishna begins to talk to himself, 'Kahbo – will you eat?' and then, childlike, he goes on eating one *jelabi* after another. He feels happy.

One day Maharishi Devendranath Tagore invited Sri Ramakrishna to the annual meeting of the Brahmo Samaj. Devendranath Tagore said to the saint, "You must come dressed in *dhoti* and in *chaddar*. Why, because I cannot bear to see any one speak ill of you, because you are improperly dressed." And what answer does the saint give? The saint said, "I do not want to attend this Annual meeting. Why, because I do not want to be dressed like a civilised Babu." His childlike soul rose above the conventions of so-called civilisation.

Totapuri came to him and said, "Shall I teach you Vedanta?" And like a child, Ramakrishna replied, "Wait, let me first ask the Mother." He went into the temple. He spoke to the Divine Mother. Then he came back and said, "Teach me, Mother permits me." A *pandit* came to him and put to him this question, "Tell me, tell me, O saint of God, what is the difference between the knower, the knowledge and the object known?" And Sri Ramakrishna said, "I do not know the niceties of knowledge. I only know one thing – that God is my Mother and I am Her child."

Sri Ramakrishna always thought of himself as a child of the Mother Divine. People called him their Guru but he said again and again, "I am not a guru. I am a child of the Mother Divine. The word guru pricks me like a thorn." Sri Ramakrishna who never liked to be called a guru, or a teacher, is acclaimed today as a world guru. All over the world there are so many who look upon him as their guru, their teacher.

Sri Ramakrishna had the same love for agnostics and atheists, as he had for believers. One day an agnostic came to meet him. This man held a master's degree of the Calcutta University. And this agnostic spoke frankly to Sri Ramakrishna concerning his disbelief and the restlessness of the mind. He confessed to Sri Ramakrishna, "I cannot pray to God, because there is no proof concerning the existence of God." Sri Ramakrishna did not despise him, he did not turn him out. Instead Sri Ramakrishna taught him an agnostic prayer. The Master said to him, "I suppose you will have no objection to offering a prayer like this. Pray to God, say to Him, 'O God if dost Thou really exist, listen to my prayer.' When you do this you will find that you will be helped. The gentleman felt that he would have no objection to offering such a prayer. He was asked to come again. And after some days when he returned to Sri Ramakrishna, he was a changed man. He touched the master's feet and said with tears in his eyes, "You have saved me."

The very first dimension of life, lived in God is breadth. Be broad-minded. Do not imprison yourself in creeds and in dogmas. My revered master said to us again and again, "Creeds are broken reeds and dogmas divide. The essence of religion is life – a life of self-realisation, a life of new awakening, self effacement, a life of sympathy, a life of simplicity, a life of sacrifice."

During his lifetime, Sri Ramakrishna was worshipped as an *avatara purusha* – an incarnation of the Divine. It is said that his small room in the Dakshineshwar temple was like a miniature Parliament of Religions, where men of all faiths congregated, to seek his blessings. Through parables, metaphors and songs, he taught them deep religious truths.

In April 1885, the first symptoms of throat cancer were noticed in him. After a terrible, physical ordeal, he attained *mahasamadhi* on August 16, 1886. He left behind him his wife, the Holy Mother Ma Saradamani, and a devoted band of disciples led by Swami Vivekananda, who would carry on his spiritual legacy.

This great spiritual heritage lives on, in the Ramakrishna Math, which is committed to spreading his ideals.

Sayings of Sri Ramakrishna Paramahansa

"Unalloyed love of God is the essential thing. All else is unreal."

* * * * *

"I have now come to a stage of realisation in which I see that God is walking in every human form and manifesting Himself alike through the sage and the sinner, the virtuous and the vicious. Therefore, when I meet different people I say to myself, "God in the form of the saint, God in the form of the sinner, God in the form of the righteous, God in the form of the unrighteous."

* * * * *

"One should not think, 'My religion alone is the right path and other religions are false.' God can be realised by means of all paths. It is enough to have sincere yearning for God. Infinite are the paths and infinite the opinions."

* * * * *

"God is in all men, but all men are not in God; that is why we suffer."

* * * * *

"Many are the names of God and infinite the forms through which He may be approached."

* * * * *

"What are you to do when you are placed in the world? Give up everything to Him, resign yourself to Him, and there will be no more trouble for you. Then you will come to know that everything is done by His Will."

* * * * *

"If one has faith, one has everything."

Some Books by Sri Ramakrishna Paramahansa

- *The Gospel of Sri Ramakrishna* – by Sri Ramakrishna; Swami Nikhilananda (trans.)
- *Sri Ramakrishna Upanishad*
- *Sayings of Sri Ramakrishna*
- *Teachings of Sri Ramakrishna*
- *Tales and Parables of Sri Ramakrishna*

Some Books on Sri Ramakrishna Paramahansa

- *My Master* – Swami Vivekananda
- *Life of Ramakrishna* – Romain Rolland
- *A Short Life of Sri Ramakrishna* – Swami Tejasananda
- *Ramakrishna: His Life and Sayings* – Max Muller
- *Sri Ramakrishna: A Prophet for the New Age* – Richard Schiffman
- *Ramakrishna and His Disciples* – by Christopher Isherwood
- *Kali's Child*: The Mystical and the Erotic in the Life and Teachings of Ramakrishna – by Jeffrey J. Kripal
- *Great Swan*: Meetings with Ramakrishna – by Lex Hixon
- *Ramakrishna As We Saw Him* – by Swami Chetanananda

Baha'u'llah

Baha'u'llah is one of the greatest prophets of harmony and reconciliation humanity has known. He was rightly called the defender of the oppressed and the refuge of the poor. In his teaching the emphasis was on search after truth, the oneness of mankind, unity of religions, races and nations, unity of East and West, the reconciliation of religion and science, the eradication of prejudices and superstitions, the equality of men and women and the compulsory diffusion of knowledge.

Baha'u'llah

On November 12, 1817, a great saint, seer and prophet was born in Teheran, which was the capital of Persia (Iran) at that time. Named Mirza Hussain Ali Nuri by his loving parents, he grew up to become the Founder of what we now know as the Baha'i faith. In love and reverence, the world refers to him today as Baha'u'llah – meaning the glory of God, or the Light of God.

Baha'u'llah's mother was a pious lady, called Kadijih Khanum; his father was Mirza Buzurg, who was a prominent dignitary in the royal court. Mirza Buzurg served the Shah of Persia as a minister and then as a governor. Thus, his son was brought up in a luxurious environment.

But the young boy was not attracted by the material splendour with which he was surrounded. From his childhood, he loved to sit in silence, and think about life and its meaning. When the young boy was told the story of the massacre of innocent tribesmen in the early years of Islam, he was profoundly moved – for his was a deeply sensitive nature.

When he was very young, the family celebrated the wedding of his elder brother in a grand manner. On this occasion, a puppet show had been arranged for the entertainment of the guests, and the boy watched the show enthralled.

The story was set in a royal palace. The courtier puppets await the arrival of the king anxiously, having made grand preparations for his welcome. Some puppets sweep and mop the floor; other puppets decorate the palace with flowers; yet others lay out a red carpet for the king.

Soon, the puppet king arrives and sits on the throne. His soldiers drag a robber into the court, and request the king to punish him. Imperiously, His Majesty orders the thief's head to be severed from his body; the executioner arrives immediately with a huge butcher's knife and the robber is beheaded!

All of a sudden, a puppet messenger arrives to warn the king that enemies have entered his kingdom, and are likely to attack the palace any minute. The king orders his general to mobilise the army and prepare for war...

...And so the show went on. Young Hussain Ali watched it all in amazement, until it ended, with thunderous applause from those present.

The audience dispersed. But the young lad stood rooted to the ground, unable to take his eyes off the puppet stage.

What did he see? In a matter of minutes, the master puppeteer left the hall, carrying a small bag with him.

"Can you tell me what are you carrying in this bag?" the little boy asked him.

"All the puppets you saw on that stage a few minutes ago, are now packed into this bag," the man replied. "And in this bag they will remain until I pull them out for the next show."

Hearing this, the child was astonished. So this was what it was all about! In a flash it dawned on him that this world was also like an elaborate puppet show – and all of us are puppets, talking, laughing, planning, plotting, absorbed in our petty lives. We do not even pause for a moment to realise that the show must soon come to an end – and back to the bag we must return!

Then and there, the child made a mental resolve: life is too short; time is too precious; our sojourn upon this earth is ephemeral; therefore, I must not waste my time!

A mere puppet show was enough to make Baha'u'llah realise how illusory and transient were the trappings of earthly glory.

When Baha'u'llah was seventeen years old, his father passed away. A position at court was offered to the young man, but he turned it down, for his spiritual leanings were too strong for worldly positions.

When he was twenty-seven years old, Baha'u'llah received the message of the Bab – a new Prophet who was known as the *Mahdi* of Islam. Baha'u'llah accepted the new faith eagerly, and from then on, made it his life's mission to spread the Babi faith amongst the people. His high birth, his noble character and his power of eloquence made him highly successful as a preacher, and many were won over to the faith.

This angered the *mullahs*, who complained to the king, filling the king's ears with falsehood against Baha'u'llah. The king ordered him to be captured and thrown in prison.

Prison, in his case, was a cell in utter darkness, where not a ray of sunlight penetrated. But, during his incarceration, he had several mystical experiences. An Angel of God appeared to him in his dream and made him realise that he, Baha'u'llah, was God's messenger – the one whom the Bab had termed "He whom God shall make manifest."

He was released from prison – only to be deported to Iraq, where he arrived in 1853. For the next ten years, he lived in Baghdad, which now became the centre of the new faith. Thousands of seekers travelled from Teheran to Baghdad to see and hear the new Prophet, their new leader. He was a magnetic personality – a living, moving picture of love and compassion.

His fame and respect among the people grew; but so did the jealousy of his opponents within the Babi faith. Baha'u'llah left Baghdad to go and live alone in the hilly regions of Kurdistan, for he had no wish to cause divisions within the Babi community.

For two long years, he lived the life of a *Dervish* in the mountains; but even there, his learning and wisdom attracted the attention of very many seekers. During this time, he wrote some of his most notable books.

In the meanwhile, without the presence of a true spiritual leader, the Babi community became disheartened and divided. Baha'u'llah was earnestly requested to return to Baghdad. Here, many of his books and revelations were published.

His rising influence in Baghdad, and the revival of the Babi community angered his enemies. Once again, he was deported – to Constantinople, in the Ottoman Empire.

Baha'u'llah left Baghdad, and he and a few of his followers spent a few days in the Garden of Ridvan, near Baghdad. It was here that Baha'u'llah declared to his companions, the secret about his revelations, and proclaimed his holy mission as a messenger of God. Even now, the Baha'is celebrate these twelve days as their sacred Festival of Ridvan. Between his mystic visions in prison and his declaration to his companions, twelve years had passed! This period was referred to as *ayyam-i-butun* – or "Days of Concealment" by Baha'u'llah himself.

Now the Prophet and his family, along with a small band of faithful followers, stayed in Constantinople. But this was not to last. For it was only the beginning of a long process which would gradually move him into further exile and deportation.

In Adrianapole where he lived for some time, his enemies even attempted to imprison him. He proclaimed the Baha'i faith and appealed to all kings and rulers asking them to accept his revelations and work together for the betterment of humanity.

From Adrianapole Baha'u'llah was deported to Akka in Palestine, and here the saint spent the final years of his life.

In 1890 the Cambridge Orientalist, Edward Granville Brown, visited Baha'u'llah and described him thus:

> ... The face of him on whom I gazed, I can never forget, though I can not describe it. Those piercing eyes seemed to read one's very soul; Power and authority set on the ample brow... I bowed myself before one who is the object of a devotion and love which kings might envy and emperors sigh for in vain!

On May 9, 1982 Baha'u'llah contracted a fever which eventually took his life on May 29, 1982.

Baha'u'llah taught the underlying unity of all the worlds' religions, including Judaism, Christianity, Zoroastrianism, Islam and Hinduism. (His son and spiritual heir, actually hailed both Sri Krishna and Buddha as true prophets). Baha'u'llah advocated compulsory education for girls, asserting that in his religion "women are equal to men"; he urged his followers to avoid national and religious prejudices, and insisted that love of all humanity was far superior to narrow nationalism. Baha'is believe that the Buddhist prophecy, that *Maitreya* will usher in a new society of tolerance and love, has indeed been fulfilled by Baha'u'llah's teachings on world peace.

Sayings of Baha'u'llah

"So powerful is the light of unity that it can illuminate the whole earth."

* * * * *

"It is not for him to pride himself who loveth his own country, but rather for him who loveth the whole world. The earth is but one country and mankind its citizens."

* * * * *

"God's purpose in sending His Prophets unto men is twofold. The first is to liberate the children of men from the darkness of ignorance, and guide them to the light of true understanding. The second is to ensure the peace and tranquility of mankind, and provide all the means by which they can be established."

* * * * *

"Blessed and happy is he that ariseth to promote the best interests of the peoples and kindreds of the earth."

* * * * *

"If haste is harmful, inertness and indolence are a thousand times worse. A middle course is best..."

* * * * *

"Cleanse ye your eyes, so that ye behold no man as different from yourselves. See ye no strangers; rather see all men as friends."

* * * * *

"Love ye all religions and all races with a love that is true and sincere and show that love through deeds"

* * * * *

"Those who do most good use fewest words concerning their actions."

Some Books by Baha'u'llah

- Rashh-i-'Amá, 'Sprinkling from a Cloud'
- Lawh-i-Kullu'-Ta'ám, 'Tablet of All Food'
- Chahár Vádí, 'Four Valleys'
- Kalimát-i-Maknúnih, 'Hidden Words'
- Javáhiru'l-Asrár, 'Gems of Divine Mysteries'
- Asl-i-Kullu'l-Khayr, 'Words of Wisdom'
- Súrihs of Hajj, 'Tablets of Pilgrimage'
- Madínatu't-Tawhíd, 'City of Unity'
- Lawh-i-Ghulámu'l-Khuld, 'Tablet of the Eternal Youth'
- Tajallíyát, 'Effulgences'

Some Books on Baha'u'llah

- *Baha'u'llah: A Short Biography* – by Moojan Momen
- *The Story of Baha'u'llah, Promised One of All Religions* – by Druzelle Cederquist
- *Love of Baha'u'llah* – by Mehrabi
- *The Covenant of Baha'u'llah* – by Adib Taherzadeh
- *Robe of Light*: The Persian Years of the Supreme Prophet, Baha'u'llah – by David S. Ruhe
- *Baha'u'llah and the New Era* – by J. E. Esslemont
- *Baha'u'llah: the King of Glory* – by Hasan Balyuzi
- *Baha'u'llah, the Prince of Peace*: A Portrait – by David Hofman

Lord Dattatreya

*D*attatreya is held in great reverence as an Aadi Guru and a Divine incarnation of the Holy Trinity. His birth was a miraculous event; and he evolved to become a great *Brahma Gnani*, teaching great truths to seekers. Above all, he was himself a true seeker, who learnt from everything and everyone with whom he came into contact.

Lord Dattatreya

*L*et me tell you about an *acharya*, an *avatara* of the Lord, who is worshipped by many Hindus as a God. He is Lord Dattatreya, who is regarded as a Divine Incarnation of the Holy Trinity, Brahma, Shiva and Vishnu. The word Datta in Sanskrit means 'given'; and 'Atreya' signifies the lineage of the great Sage Atri. Dattatreya was 'given' to sage Atri and his wife, Anasuya, as a gift of the Gods. Dattatreya is also regarded as the *Aadi Guru* in the Nath tradition of worship.

There are many versions of the legend of Dattatreya, and each one of them is deeply symbolic and significant. I shall narrate to you the version of his story as it is told to us in the *Markandeya Purana*.

Sage Atri and his wife Anasuya were a pious and a devoted couple; Anasuya was an ideal *rishi patni*, who was a tremendous source of support to her husband in his spiritual practices. A few *rishis* who had met the couple, happened to speak very highly of her faith and devotion to her husband. Indeed, they praised her to the skies.

This came to the notice of Goddesses Lakshmi, Parvati and Saraswati. When they heard of Anasuya and her great qualities as a *pativrata*, they begged their husbands – Vishnu, Shiva and Brahma – to put Anasuya to the test, so that they may see how devoted she was.

The Holy Trinity of the Gods assumed the role of mendicant *sanyasis* and went to Atri's *ashram*; there, they begged for food with the traditional words: *Bhavati bikshaam dehi*. As you know, India's ancient scriptures tell us that it is our duty to feed those who come to our door. *Athiti devo bhava*; the guest is the equivalent of God. And when they happen to be ascetics who are obliged to live on food that is begged as *biksha*, it is incumbent upon the lady of the house to offer them food, even if it happens to be the last morsel in the house! Accordingly, the pious and devout Anasuya came out immediately, to offer them food. But the three mendicants laid an impossible condition before her: they would not accept food at her hands, unless she served them without any clothes on her person – in other words, completely naked.

This might sound shocking to us in the modern age! But in those days of *Tretayuga*, people were made of sterner stuff, and would analyse the reasons behind such strange requests. So did Anasuya. Being the perfect *grahasti*, she knew it was her sacred duty to feed the mendicants, who had begged food from her; in this sense, they would be like her children, and she, who offered them food, would be in their mother's position. But the strange condition they had laid, revealed that they were no ordinary mendicants. Above all, so true and faithful was her devotion to her husband, that Anasuya was certain that no harm or shame would ever come to her. She decided to accept the strange condition and offer food to the visitors.

She meditated on the form of her husband, took refuge at his feet, and sprinkled over the three *Sanyasins,* a few drops of water which were used for washing the feet of her husband. The moment Anasuya did this, the Gods who were standing before her, turned into tiny infants, mewling and crying at her doorstep. Overjoyed at this Divine Miracle, Anasuya picked the infants up and fed them with her own milk. When the babes were fed, she put them to sleep. Upon her husband's return, she narrated the story to him, and he was delighted and proud to hear of her noble conduct. The couple decided that they would keep the 'divine children' with them – and such was the Sage's *taposhakti,* that the Holy Trinity stayed in his *ashram* as three tiny, helpless infants.

However, alarm bells began to ring for their wives, who quickly descended to the earth to explain the *leela* to Anasuya. They freely acknowledged that she was indeed, a true *pativrata* and begged her to return their consorts to them. Instantly, sage Atri turned the infants into their original form – and Vishnu, Shiva and Brahma blessed the holy couple and granted them a boon of their choice.

Anasuya prayed that she should be blessed with a son, who would be the very incarnation of the Holy Trinity – and by this Divine Boon was born Dattatreya.

When Dattatreya attained manhood, he was gentle, peaceful and amiable. As he had the grace of the Tri-Murtis, and as he was a great *Jnani*, all rishis and ascetics worshipped him.

While the Adinath *Sampradaya* regards Dattatreya as the Lord of yoga and the first Guru, He is worshipped by millions of Hindus as a benevolent God.

Dattatreya is usually depicted with three heads, symbolising Brahma, Vishnu and Shiva – as well as past, present and future; and the three states of consciousness, waking, dreaming and dreamless sleep. He is portrayed sitting in meditation beneath an *adumbara* (wish-fulfilling) tree. In front of him are four dogs representing the Vedas.

According to the *Brahma Purana*, Dattatreya performed *tapasya* on the banks of the River Gautami, and was blessed by Shiva to become a *Brahma Gnani*. Thus, he is worshipped as *Adi Siddha*.

Dattatreya is one of the oldest deities, and mention is made of him in the *Mahabharata* and *Ramayana*. Several different sects and traditions have accepted him as an *avatar* and he continues to be worshipped widely in Maharashtra, Gujarat, Karnataka and Andhra Pradesh.

In the *Srimad Bhagawatam*, we have another fascinating reference to Lord Dattatreya, narrated by Sri Krishna to his friend Uddhava. Dattatreya, speaking to King Yadu, a great ancestor and forefather of Sri Krishna, had revealed that he had learnt invaluable lessons and precepts from each of his twenty-four *Gurus* – the different aspects of creation.

It is said that King Yadu was wonderstruck by Dattatreya's spiritual radiance and the perfect contentment and peace in which he seemed to live, and begged him to reveal the secret of his happiness, as well as the name of the Guru who had imparted the same to him.

To this, the illustrious *avatara purusha* replied, "The Self alone is my Guru. Yet, I have learned wisdom from twenty-four other sources. Therefore, I regard them too, as my Gurus." He then mentioned the names of his twenty-four Gurus, and spoke of the wisdom they had bestowed on him.

Who were these fascinating group of twenty-four great teachers?

They were:

Earth, water, air, sky, fire, the sun, the moon, a pigeon, a python, the ocean, a moth, a honeybee, an elephant, a honey-gatherer, a deer, a fish, a dancing girl, an osprey, a child, an arrow-maker, a maiden, a serpent, a spider and a wasp.

What was the nature of the wisdom that these Gurus imparted to Dattatreya?

1. *The Earth* taught him the qualities of patience, forbearance and doing good to others.

From the moment we get up from sleep, we stand upon the earth, we stamp upon it, we tread upon it, we jump and walk upon it. The earth puts up with it all – it puts up with billions upon billions of people like us and continues to support us.

The trees that grow upon the earth share this quality with their earth mother. They provide shelter and fruits to everyone – even to those who throw stones at them.

The true seeker learns to cultivate endurance, compassion and selflessness from the earth.

2. *The Air* taught him detachment. It carries so many smells and vapours with it – good and bad – but it remains unaffected by them all.

The seeker must realise that his *atman* too, is like the air – good and bad *karmas* cannot affect its essential nature.

3. *The Sky* taught him the nature of all-pervading Brahma which is all around us, everywhere – and yet not in contact with any object.

The seeker must learn that deep within himself is the unlimited, infinite space of pure awareness that is the Self.

4. *Water* taught him the lesson of purity. Water quenches thirst; its quality is sweet, its feel is smooth; water also washes, cleanses and purifies.

The seeker should aspire to become like the water – cleansing, purifying and thirst-quenching in the service of others.

5. *Fire* taught him about the quality of illumination and effulgence. Fire burns everything; it gives out light and removes darkness.

   The seeker must be like the fire which destroys all evil, and continues to shed radiance. His self-knowledge should dispel the darkness of ignorance around him.

6. *The Sun* taught him the unity of all Being. Although there is one Sun in the sky, its reflection is found in various forms in reservoirs, rivers and even in the smallest earthern pots.

   The seeker learns from the sun that the *jivatmas* are but reflections of the one great *Paramatma*.

7. *The Moon* taught him that Reality is unchanging – while appearances are illusory. The moon seems to wax and wane in our sight, but it is ever the same. So too, the Self is perfect and changeless – while man rises or falls according to his actions in life.

8. *A Pigeon* taught him an unforgettable lesson on worldly attachments which often become entanglements for the soul.

   The sage saw a family of pigeons living on a tree. One day, the father and mother had left their young ones behind and flown out to gather food. Finding the young ones alone, a hunter spread his net and caught the young birds. When the parents returned and saw their young ones ensnared, they were disconsolate. In profound grief, overwhelmed by her inability to save her children, the mother threw herself into the net. Seeing her, the father followed her example – and thus the whole family was trapped in misery. Perhaps, if the parent-birds had applied themselves to the problem, they could have found ways and means to save their little ones. But, as it happened, all of them perished at the hands of the hunter.

The seeker must learn that attachment is the root cause of all worldly bondage. Our worldly entanglements only lead to misery.

9. *The Python* taught him that God provides for all creatures, according to their needs. The python is a gigantic creature which cannot move about nimbly to gather its food; yet God, in His wisdom and mercy, sends food to this creature.

The aspirant must learn from the python the spirit of surrender and acceptance, in the complete faith that God will deal with us according to our *karmic* needs.

10. *The Ocean* taught him the quality of tranquility, of being unmoved by all incidents and accidents of life. Just as the ocean remains in place even as hundreds of rivers and waterways pour into it, so the soul must rest within its own bounds, in its own sense of fullness.

The aspirants must learn profundity and depth from the ocean, that he may remain calm and still and deep, as the tides of change rise and flow all around him.

11. *The Moth* taught him two valuable lessons; when man becomes dazzled by earthly enchantments, he will perish by his own desires even as the moth rushes into the flame, to be destroyed. A higher and more profound lesson is that when it seeks light, it enters the light and allows itself, its individuality to be merged with the light.

    From the moth, the seeker must learn to keep away from self-destructive passions and desires, while aspiring to become One with God.

12. *The Honeybee* taught him that the nectar of life is gathered from different sources. Similarly a *sanyasi* begs for a little food from each household that he may not become a burden on any one individual.

    The seeker must learn that spiritual qualities can be imbibed from all sorts of experiences. He must learn to absorb and assimilate his experiences and gather the honey of the spiritual wisdom from all these sources.

13. *The Elephant* taught him to be wary of temptation and lust. Lured by the sight of the female elephant, the male elephant walks foolishly into the trap laid by men — falling into a pit cleverly covered with grass so as to make it trip and fall.

    The aspirant must learn from this that he must practise self-control and avoid being lured by lust and passion.

14. *The Honey-gatherer* is a bird which is a kind of robber among the fauna and flora. After the

industrious bees have worked hard to gather and store the honey in the hives, they relax, hoping to enjoy the fruit of their labour later. At this time the honey-gatherer arrives and steals all the honey, leaving very little for the bees.

The lesson that the seeker must learn is not to hoard and preserve wealth for an unknown, unseen future – for that future may never be ours! It is better we utilise our wealth for the present benefit of us and others, instead of hoarding excessive wealth beyond our needs.

15. *The Deer* is often lured and trapped by hunters using a strange device – they play upon drums creating a kind of music that enthralls the deer. It pursues the music, walking into the trap laid by the hunters.

For the aspirant, this 'enchanting' music represents the fleeting, alluring sensory pleasures that the world has to offer. When we are lured by these pleasures, we have no time to spare for the higher, loftier aspects of our life. Therefore, we must resist the 'call' of the senses.

16. *The Fish* taught Dattatreya a valuable lesson: its eyes are always open; its swims about freely in the water; and yet, it allows itself to be 'hooked' miserably, by 'swallowing the bait' that is put out to catch it! The bait is a pathetic worm – and the fish falls for the sake of this little worm, suffering horrible pain and then a miserable death.

The aspirant should learn that he should not 'rise to the bait' by yielding to every temptation that is presented, to him. More particularly, he should guard against greed for the wrong kinds of food.

17. *A Dancing-girl* named Pingala taught the hermit another valuable lesson. She depended for her livelihood on wealthy 'customers' who would pay her in return for her company. One day, she waited and waited for her rich clients – and not one of them appeared. At first she gave in to hopelessness – but out of this grew her sense of dispassion. She became determined to devote all her effort and attention to God, rather than to her earthly patrons. The 'treasure' she would earn by this would be far more valuable than the material wealth her customers brought her.

The seeker too, must learn that worldly ambition is less worthwhile than higher aspirations. Instead of directing our desire towards people and treasures which come and go, we should direct it towards God – for in His Love is our salvation.

18. *An Osprey* taught Dattatreya to guard against the sense of greed and covetousness. This bird found a piece of meat and grabbed it in his beak. As he flew away with it, he was pursued by vultures and hawks and other birds of prey. Feeling threatened by their pursuit he dropped the piece of meat he was carrying and lo and behold, the birds of prey

quit following him and swooped down on the meat instead!

From this the seeker must learn that the man who covets worldly wealth and pleasures must face enmity, hostility and unforeseen dangers. When he 'lets go' of these, he attains peace and tranquility.

19. *A Child*, an infant, taught him the value of carefree existence and true happiness. When you scold him or speak harshly to him, the child cries; but he forgets your anger and harshness very soon, and smiles at you happily. He does not harbour any grudge or resentment; he holds no ill-will against anyone for long.

The aspirant must also cultivate this quality of child-like innocence and simplicity, which will enable him to be positive and cheerful at all times, with all people.

20. *A Poor maiden* was husking paddy, when visitors bringing a proposal of marriage for her, came to see her parents. They were seated in the outer room, while her chores kept her busy in the kitchen. She realised that the many bangles and bracelets she wore on her arm were jingling and making too much noise; embarrassed, she removed a few of them – but the noise did not abate. One by one, she removed all of them until there was just one bangle on each wrist. Now, she continued peacefully with her work.

The many 'bonds' and 'attachments' of this world only add to the stress and clamour of life. They breed dependence. Likewise, multiplicity of wants and constant company of crowds hampers us from self-realisation. Solitude, breaking away from crowds, will help us move towards our goal unhindered.

21. *The Arrow-maker* was a role-model of focus and concentration. His mind, his eyes and his hands were all directed towards his chosen task of forging arrows and directing them at their target. When the King passed by him in a long, royal procession, the arrow-maker did not even notice them; such was his concentration and focus.

    The aspirant too, must learn to practise his *sadhana* with one-pointed mind, *ekagrita*. Our soul should be like the arrow which is directed at the target of Liberation – *Moksha*. We must not let our attention be distracted by the shouts and shows of this world.

22. *A Serpent* taught Dattatreya the lesson of non-possession and independence. A serpent does not make a home for itself; it dwells in holes dug by other animals. And a serpent lives on its own – not in groups or with other serpents.

    An aspirant must also learn to do without possessions and attachment.

23. *The Spider* spins its web out of its own saliva, and sometimes, he himself gets entangled in it. We

must guard against getting entangled in the web of our own desires. Also, the spider reminds us that this vast Universe is a web of illusion created by *Brahman*. The world is not material, not real; it is made up of the substance of God.

24. *The Wasp*, in its life-cycle, passes from the egg, through the larva and the pupa to its final form. It teaches us not to identify with the body – our physical form – and realise that we are the *atman*, the immortal soul, which is ever ready to fly towards God and Liberation!

These were the twenty-four Gurus of Dattatreya – and he himself acknowledged them as such.

May we be inspired by his illustrious example! Let us also have open minds; let us be free from prejudice and intolerance; let us learn from all; let us learn in every way we can!

Sayings of Dattatreya

"Verily the one Self is all, free from differentiation and non-differentiation. Neither can it be said, 'It is' nor 'It is not.' What a great mystery."

* * * * *

"*That God who is the Self in* all impersonal and changeless, like unto space, by nature purity itself verily, verily, that *I am*."

* * * * *

"The mind is as space, embracing all. I am beyond mind. In Reality, *mind has no independent existence.*"

* * * * *

"Oh my mind, why do you range in delusion like a ghost? Know *Atman* to be above duality and be happy."

* * * * *

"How can the supreme Reality be described, since It is neither white nor any other colour, has no qualities such as sound, and is beyond voice and mind?"

* * * * *

"I am without beginning and without end. Never was I bound. By nature pure, taintless is my Self. This I know for sure."

* * * * *

"As a volume of water poured into water is inseparably united with water, so, I perceive, matter and spirit are one."

* * * * *

"He who has conquered the feelings of pleasure, wrath, avarice, attachment, vanity and aversion, this one is peace itself, and free from all pride."

* * * * *

"When my mind began to meditate on You, it lost all interest in objects. When my tongue began to praise You it lost the power of praising others. I forgot my three great sins."

Some Books by Dattatreya

- *Avadhuta Gita*
- *Yoga shastra of Dattatreya*

Some Books on Dattatreya

- *Shri Guru Charitra*
- *Shri Datta Prabodh*
- *Shri Guruleelamrut*
- *Shri Datta Mahatmya*
- *Shri Datta Charitrasar*
- *Sahyadrivarnat*
- *Dattatreya: The Way and the Goal* – by Jaya Chamaraja Wadiyar
- *Dattatreya: The Immortal Guru, Yogin and Avatara*: A Study of the Transformative and Inclusive Character of a Multi-Faceted Hindu Deity – by Antonio Rigopoulos
- *Dattatreya the Absolute* – by Sachchidananda

Helen Keller

Helen Keller is a miracle of our age. She had the insight of a seer. She foretold a bright future for mankind. If the greedy, she pointed out, thought better, the needy would be able to live better. Afflicted with severe disabilities of vision, speech and hearing, she overcame these handicaps with her extraordinary determination and strength of spirit, giving a whole new meaning to the term we use now – a *specially* abled person.

Helen Keller

All of us love to share our thoughts and feelings with our friends and relatives, our near and dear ones. Can you imagine what would be our condition if, we were unable to express ourselves? What if we were unable to speak? What if we were doomed to live in a world of continuous silence, unable to hear anything? What if we were absolutely unable to see? How we love to see the rising sun, the moon and stars, the lush green lawns, the tall mountains, the bubbling brooks, the sweet, smiling, innocent faces of babes, the limitless sky, the huge expanse of the deep blue oceans, and all our loved ones! But what if we were doomed to live forever in an agonizing world of darkness? What if we were unable to see and hear and speak?

Let me tell you about someone who was without sight, speech and hearing – yet was able to overcome all these handicaps with stupendous effort and an indomitable will. Her name was Helen Keller. She was born on June 27, 1880, in America. Her father was a Captain in the Civil War. She was born a normal child. She could see and hear. But when she was a year and a half old, she fell very sick. Her parents were afraid that she would not survive. Although she recovered from the illness, it left an indelible effect on her. Helen would never be able to see. She would never be able to hear, nor would she ever be able to utter a single word. As she grew up, this little child was bewildered, traumatised by what had happened to her. Why could she not hear her father and mother's voice or see them? Her condition was similar to that of a wild animal.

Her parents tried hard to communicate with her, but were helpless. They loved Helen dearly. They wanted to give her the best medical care. They took her to the best doctor in Baltimore. After examining her, the doctor solemnly stated, "Helen will never be able to see and hear. We can do nothing to help her." Dejected, the parents returned home.

Helen lived a miserable life. One day she locked up the kitchen where her mother was working. The poor mother banged at the door from the inside, and Helen just stood outside, laughing. Though she did not hear the sounds of the loud banging on the door, she could feel the sound vibrations, and that made her happy.

On another occasion, when her little sister was sleeping in the cradle, Helen overturned the cradle. It was fortunate that her mother who was sitting nearby, noticed it and immediately grabbed the tiny baby in her arms, or else the baby would have been seriously injured.

On yet another occasion, Helen spilt water on her clothes. The clothes were soaking wet. She wondered how she could dry them. As she was an intelligent child, she decided that the heat from the fire would dry them. She stood near the fire and attempted to dry her dress. But after a while, as her dress was still wet, Helen drew still closer to the fire and her clothes caught fire! A maid standing nearby quickly wrapped a blanket around her and extinguished the fire. Else, Helen would have been burnt to ashes.

Her parents sincerely prayed to God to show them the way. Finally, their prayers were answered and a teacher called Annie Sullivan, offered to train Helen. Annie Sullivan's life was also in a way, unique. She had been through several illnesses and survived them all. She was familiar with pain. She was aware of poverty and hunger, so her heart moved out in sympathy to Helen and she resolved to help Helen and bring about a change in her life. Annie started off by writing different words for different things on the child's hand. Helen, in return, started memorising those words. In her autobiography, Helen Keller writes, "The day I could identify things by their name was, indeed memorable... I don't think any one must have ever experienced so much joy." Just a little before her eighth birthday, both her mother and Annie, took Helen to Massachusetts. Helen carried with herself her favourite doll and some books in Braille. When the mother and Annie wanted to rest, Helen would start reading.

"Why do you love books?" Helen was asked. "Because they describe to me things I cannot see and they never feel tired or troubled, like human beings."

Newspapers now started carrying stories about Helen Keller. People were amazed to know how a deaf, dumb and blind child could actually read and communicate. Many came to visit them.

Helen came to know that in the same school in which she studied, there was a blind and deaf boy named Tommy Stringer. He had no family and no one to teach him and take care of him.

Helen's heart immediately went out to Tommy. She wanted to help him. Helen raised some money to enable little Tommy to go to school. In due course, Tommy became Helen's best friend.

When Helen turned ten, she learnt that a blind and deaf girl in Norway had been able to use her own voice and speak clearly. Helen's heart was filled with a new hope.

At the age of 10, Helen had another teacher, whose name was Miss Fuller. She taught Helen how to talk. Helen being intelligent, opened her mouth like her teacher, stuck her tongue out and made her first sound. On the very first day itself, Miss Fuller was successful in teaching her six letters of the English language. She was able to pronounce the letters – M, P, A, S, T, I.

Helen practised very sincerely and the day dawned when she could also speak. At the age of 14, Dr. Humason gave Helen special lessons in speaking and reading. She joined The Wright Humason School.

In New York, Helen made a special friend – Mark Twain. Mark Twain narrated funny stories to Helen. He loved to make her laugh. Once he remarked, "I lecture to thousands of people, but Helen is my best audience." However, Helen's father fell ill and it became difficult for the family to pay for Helen's School fees. Mark Twain encouraged her and along with his friends, raised funds for her schooling.

Helen worked very hard. She learnt to use a Braille typewriter and finally she passed her school examination and entered the Radcliffe College. In college Helen was elected the Vice President of her class. English was her favourite subject. She wrote such good themes that some of them were even published. In fact, a magazine paid her to write the thrilling story of her own life. Helen was happy that she could learn and also earn.

In June 1904, Helen graduated from college.

Now Helen Keller took more speech and voice lessons and even started lecturing. She practised for many hours so that she could perform well.

She travelled all over the country, addressing audiences. Between her trips she wrote books and articles for various magazines.

At college, her professor had said to her, "God has granted you a priceless gift. You have a unique way of looking at things, and expressing them in a wondrous manner. You must therefore, write your autobiography, for it will inspire many."

Helen Keller wrote her autobiography. People read her book. They marvelled at her confidence and courage. It was indeed, remarkable that a person who could not hear, speak or see was able to reach across to people around the world and inspire them!

She travelled to Europe and Africa. On coming to Asia, she started a school for the blind. She started many institutions for the service of the blind. During World War II, in which many soldiers were wounded, Helen went and counseled them. She said to them, "Look at me. In spite of my disabilities, I am living a full life. You, too can do likewise."

Helen Keller proved that not only could the blind lead the blind but also lead those who could see, by giving them a new vision of life. Wherever Helen Keller went she would give this one message, the same that Gurudev Sadhu Vaswani gave us, "True light is the light of the *atman*, the soul." If you do not see that light, then you are verily blind. Hence always kindle the light of the *atman* (Soul). Before doing any work, think for a moment. Ask yourself, "Will what I am doing lead to the illumination of the *atman?*" Only then let me proceed.

Let us salute this great messiah of the physically challenged, the differently abled, who through her great power of insight and intuition, broke through the barriers of her disabilities. She bore witness to the teaching that, we must never give up and trust the eternal power within each one of us!

Sayings of Helen Keller

"Alone we can do so little; together we can do so much."

* * * * *

"Although the world is full of suffering, it is also full of the overcoming of it."

* * * * *

"As selfishness and complaint pervert the mind, so love with its joy clears and sharpens the vision."

* * * * *

"As the eagle was killed by the arrow winged with his own feather, so the hand of the world is wounded by its own skill."

* * * * *

"Avoiding danger is no safer in the long run than outright exposure. The fearful are caught as often as the bold."

* * * * *

"Character cannot be developed in ease and quiet. Only through experience of trial and suffering can the soul be strengthened, ambition inspired, and success achieved."

* * * * *

"Death is no more than passing from one room into another. But there's a difference for me, you know. Because in that other room I shall be able to see."

* * * * *

"Everything has its wonders, even darkness and silence, and I learn, whatever state I may be in, therein to be content."

* * * * *

"Faith is the strength by which a shattered world shall emerge into the light."

* * * * *

"I do not want the peace which passeth understanding, I want the understanding which bringeth peace."

* * * * *

"I seldom think about my limitations, and they never make me sad. Perhaps there is just a touch of yearning at times; but it is vague, like a breeze among flowers."

Some Books by Helen Keller

- *The Story of My Life*
- *Optimism*
- *Seek Happiness*: Inspiring Reflections from Helen Keller
- *The World I Live In* – by Helen Keller and Roger Shattuck
- *To Love This Life* – Quotations by Helen Keller
- *Out of the Dark*: Essays, Letters, And Addresses on Physical And Social Vision
- *My Religion*
- *The Open Door*
- *Teacher: Anne Sullivan Macy*: a tribute by the foster-child of her mind: Hellen
- *Helen Keller: Her Socialist Years*: Writings and Speeches – by Helen Keller and Philip S. Foner

Some Books on Helen Keller

- *Helen Keller* (Scholastic Biography) – by Margaret Davidson and Wendy Watson
- *Who Was Helen Keller?* – by Gare Thompson and Nancy Harrison
- *Helen Keller* (Young Yearling Book) – by Stewart Graff and Polly Anne Graff
- *Helen Keller: A Life* – by Dorothy Herrmann
- *Helen Keller: From Tragedy to Triumph* (The Childhood of Famous Americans Series) – by Katharine Wilkie and Robert Doremus
- *Helen Keller* (Rookie Biographies) – by Sean Dolan
- *Helen Keller: A Determined Life* (Snapshots: Images of People and Places in History) – by Elizabeth MacLeod
- *The World At Her Fingertips*: Story of Helen Keller – by Joan Dash

Leo Tolstoy

Leo Tolstoy was born an aristocrat. He grew up in the lap of luxury. He was celebrated as one of Russia's greatest novelists. But, by a remarkable transformation of the spirit, he became a *rishi*, a *Brahma Gnani*, who turned his back upon material wealth and selfish pleasures, to devote his life to the ideals of the *Sermon on The Mount*. He is revered today as a holy saint of Russia. Long before Mahatma Gandhi developed the idea of non-cooperation, Tolstoy had worked on the idea of non-participation. Gandhi referred to Tolstoy as Mahatma Tolstoy and drew inspiration from his life and teaching. Both Tolstoy and Mahatma Gandhi were messengers of truth and non-violence.

Leo Tolstoy

This is a life story of a prophet who, in his own lifetime, was admired by an unending stream of people. His home became a place of pilgrimage for people who came from various parts of the country to have a glimpse of his face, to hear his voice, to listen to his words of wisdom, to watch him in his daily work, to touch the hem of his rough peasant garment. Every sermon he gave, every word he uttered, every incident, even if it was a trivial one, was captured in shorthand. These were later printed in many volumes.

Nearly twenty three thousand books have been written about this man and his work. His own writings are compiled in hundreds of volumes. He studied life in all its multi-hued colours; he missed out nothing; he reviewed philosophy, art, literature, religion and the problems of social and political life – and on all that he touched, he left his brilliant mark. He was none other than Count Leo Tolstoy.

Tolstoy was born in an aristocratic family, in his father's estate, on August 28, 1828, in a huge mansion with 42 rooms. Wealth and luxury surrounded him:

but when there came upon him the great change of heart, this great transformation – I call it "re-birth in this birth" – he stripped himself of his worldly goods and the luxury in which he was cradled and he wore the rough clothes of a peasant: he took up the plough to till the land; he made his shoes with his own hands: he swept his own room and he ate the simple food of the peasants. In his book *Confessions* startling revelations are made. He tells us how, in his youth, he lived a "dirty, vicious life" – a life of wildness and mindless pleasure. What sins are there that he did not commit? The list of deplorable deeds includes drinking, dueling, – even murder! In his early years, he had revelled in pleasures of the married life. In later years, he strove to conquer the flesh: he tried to be a true disciple of Jesus: he became a holy saint of Russia.

He fared badly in college and his teachers despaired of him. "We are unable to put anything in his thick skull," they would complain. And 30 years later, this same person wrote two of the world's greatest novels, *War and Peace* and *Anna Karenina*.

Leo Tolstoy married Sophie, and they lived happily for almost half a century. She had been a wonderful companion and a valuable secretary to him in his creative writing efforts. But when his life changed, his attitude to society also changed with it – and they had to part ways! In their old age, she would request him to read out love poems that he had written to her, 40 years ago, when they were both madly in love with each other. As he read those beautiful passages, both of them wept profusely, for those happy days were no more.

"The tragedy of Tolstoy" was in his marriage. He was a *Rishi,* a sage, and his wife was a "society" woman. She loved luxury and he was a prophet of the simple life. She loved to amass riches, and to him, private wealth was a sin. She believed in force and he in the Law of Love. He and she were in constant clash with each other. It was a clash of ideals, not a conflict of personalities. His longing to escape his home grew and at the age of 82, he left his "home", which had become, to him, a prison of unhappiness. He fled from his wife into the cold and darkness of a lonely world not knowing where he was going. Eleven days later he caught pneumonia and died at a wayside station-house. The last words he wrote in his diary were "Escape, escape!" But to the last he retained his faith in the Divine purpose of life. "God will arrange everything," he said before he passed on! And his last words were, "To seek – always to seek!"

Tolstoy's daughter acted as his secretary during the last years of his life. She was with him when he died in a lonely Russian railway station-house surrounded by the peasants whom he loved and in whose service he had given away all his lands. She wrote a book, called *The Tragedy of Tolstoy.*

Tolstoy became a prophet of *ahimsa* long before Gandhi attracted attention. One of the important influences in Gandhi's revolution was the life and thoughts of Tolstoy, others being the *Ramayana,* the New Testament, the Gita, the *Upanishads,* the writings of Carlyle, Washington, Ruskin and Neizsche's *Thus Spake Zarathustra*. Long before Gandhi developed the idea of "non-cooperation", Tolstoy spoke of "non-participation"; and both Tolstoy and Gandhi have borne witness to the message of *ahimsa* declared by Buddha and Christ. You may remember, that Gandhi's model farm in South Africa was actually called Tolstoy Farm!

Humanity still is young; and I believe, some day *ahimsa* must replace violence and an International Parliament must replace aggressive nation cults; or this "age of science" will be no better than an age of slaughter; and civilisation will perish in a pool of blood.

At the height of his fame as a distinguished writer and a respected thinker, Tolstoy turned his back upon the fashionable society of Moscow and went to live on his estate. But he did not wish to live the life of a wealthy land owner. His aim was to serve his peasants, to make their living conditions better. He began to realise that the hope of civilisation was in simplification. He now hated luxury. That servants should wait on him and that his daughter should drink tea in muslin dresses, disgusted him! "The life", he says, "of rich and learned men not only became repulsive but lost all meaning whatsoever." And again he wrote, "The life of our circle of society not only repelled me but lost all meaning." Tolstoy now dropped all titles, "Count" and "Your Excellency". He cultivated love for manual labour. He worked at hay-making, ploughing, reaping, wood-cutting. He engaged a shoe-maker to teach him how to make boots. He preached against private property. He began to realise that happiness had nothing to do with externals, but was an inner experience. To his wife, he wrote: "I cannot help repeating that our happiness cannot, in the least, depend on what we lose or acquire but upon what we ourselves are. If we left our child a million Roubles, would he be happy? Therefore, the question about how much our income shrinks, cannot occupy me!"

He studied the Bible, the Koran and the sacred texts of the Buddhists, in his search for the meaning of life. He found what he was looking for, in the fourth chapter of St. Mathew's Gospel – in Jesus's Sermon on the Mount. Here he found the only doctrine which satisfied him, and from here, he adopted his cardinal precepts of life: Do not be angry. Do not bind yourself by unnecessary oaths. Do not resist evil by violence. Love your enemies. Practise personal chastity. This was his new gospel, his new commandments, and he preached these precepts with the faith and conviction of a new apostle.

Tolstoy never really retired. Age and failing health did not affect his spirit and his inner vision for the future. He made the world a richer place, for he lived as he taught. And, to the last, he remained "a friend of the unfriended poor".

Tolstoy lives on, in the hearts of millions, even today.

Sayings of Leo Tolstoy

"A man can live and be healthy without killing animals for food; therefore, if he eats meat, he participates in taking animal life merely for the sake of his appetite."

* * * * *

"All happy families resemble one another, each unhappy family is unhappy in its own way."

* * * * *

"And all people live, not by reason of any care they have for themselves, but by the love for them that is in other people."

* * * * *

"Art is not a handicraft, it is the transmission of feeling the artist has experienced."

* * * * *

"Even in the valley of the shadow of death, two and two do not make six."

* * * * *

"Everyone thinks of changing the world, but no one thinks of changing himself."

* * * * *

"Faith is the sense of life, that sense by virtue of which man does not destroy himself, but continues to live on. It is the force whereby we live."

* * * * *

"Love is life. All, everything that I understand, I understand only because I love. Everything is, everything exists, only because I love. Everything is united by it alone. Love is God, and to die means that I, a particle of love, shall return to the general and eternal source."

* * * * *

"The two most powerful warriors are patience and time."

* * * * *

"There is no greatness where there is no simplicity, goodness and truth."

Some Books by Leo Tolstoy

- War and Peace
- Anna Karenina
- The Kingdom Of God Is Within You
- The Kreutzer Sonata and Other Stories
- Hadji Murad
- The Death of Ivan Ilych
- Christ's Christianity
- Bethink Yourselves!
- The Complete Works of Count Tolstoy
- Life
- The Man who was Dead
- Resurrection
- A Confession
- Master and Man

Some Books on Leo Tolstoy

- Tolstoy – by A. N. Wilson
- Tolstoy – by Ernest Joseph Simmons
- Leo Tolstoy – by William Woodin Rowe
- Leo Tolstoy – by Gilbert Keith Chesterton, George Herbert Perris, Edward Garnett
- Tolstoy – by Henri Troyat and Nancy Amphoux
- Leo Tolstoy – by John Collis Stewart
- Leo Tolstoy: Resident and Stranger – by Richard Gustafson
- Tolstoy: out of the Past (Cloth) – by Alexandra Tolstoy

Rabiya

Rabiya, lovingly described by Sadhu Vaswani as the 'Mira of Islam', was indeed, the Lord's Chosen One. Poverty, hardship and slavery could not shake her deep faith in God, nor could they take away her essential goodness of heart and soul. A mystic of the Divine, Rabiya was held in reverence by her contemporaries as a saint and a truly evolved soul.

Rabiya

Who is a true lover of God? He is one who has known God, seen God face to face, conversed with Him and made God part of his life. His entire life is surrendered to God. Even if he does not possess the riches of this world, he has the one prime treasure which is an unfailing, unfaltering love for God.

Such a lover always dwells in a state of true bliss, filled with love for God at all times. He longs and yearns that his heart should be filled with love – only for God, his Beloved. His desire is to serve the suffering ones. For the sake of the Beloved, such a one sacrifices his own desires. He becomes a zero, a nothing, in all circumstances. Whether he is passing through sorrow or happiness, he accepts the Will of his Beloved.

Sufi saints are true lovers of God. Their teachings tell us that each and every seeker, who walks on the path of spirituality, has to follow *seven steps*; each one has to climb these seven steps to reach the goal.

The first step is the step of deep repentance. When awakening dawns within the heart of the seeker, he realises that the body is a temple of God and must be kept pure; and he realises with regret, "Alas, I have stained my body with impure thoughts, words and deeds." But we must remember – even this feeling of repentance arises through the Grace of the Lord.

The second step is that the seeker begins to live and move and carry out his daily duties in the awareness of God's presence in his life. He is ever conscious that he should do nothing that would displease his God and his Guru.

The third step is *vairagya* – detachment. The root of all sin and suffering is attachment. Therefore, the seeker grows in the spirit of detachment.

The fourth step is that of humility. This is not being humble outwardly, but cultivating true humility of the heart. True humility is to empty the heart of all ego-sense. The true seeker considers the Beloved as everything. "I am nothing," he exclaims. "You, my Beloved, are everything!" This is the constant cry of his heart.

The fifth step is that of infinite patience. On the path of spirituality, the seeker has to pass through innumerable trials. But he has to be patient and realise that each trial, every personal suffering, is a blessing from God. Even as gold is purified in the crucible, so the true seeker evolves, grows through difficulty, pain and suffering, because he realises that whatever comes to him is a gift from God, to purify his soul and make it radiant.

The sixth step is that of surrender. At this step, the seeker completely surrenders himself to God. He performs his duties wisely and well, but hands over the result of his efforts, to God.

The seventh step is that of gratitude, of thanking God for all His infinite mercies. The seeker, in all circumstances, keeps thanking the Lord. For him, happiness lies in accepting the Will of God.

Even such a lover of God was Rabiya. Gurudev Sadhu Vaswani referred to her as the Mira of Islam.

The name 'Rabiya' itself means 'beautiful'. No one knows exactly when and where Rabiya was born. Many people believe that she was born in the year 770 A.D. and that she left the human body in the year 801 A.D.

She was born in a very poor family, as the fourth daughter to her parents. Rabiya was born in the darkness of the night. The family lived in such abject poverty that it is said, when Rabiya was born, the lamp got extinguished as it had no more oil to burn! The mother requested the father: "Please, go and borrow some oil from one of our neighbours. And we shall return it to them later. It would be good if there is some light in our house, when the baby is born." To make his wife happy, the father left the house. He went from one neighbour to another knocking the door so softly that even he could not hear the sound, leave alone the people inside the house! So naturally, no one came to open the door.

He returned home and said to his wife, "Thrice did I knock at each door, but no one opened it." And so, Rabiya the beautiful, was born in darkness.

That night the father had a dream. He heard a Divine voice saying to him, "You are not aware that a great soul has been born unto you. This girl will lead people to God, she will help them turn back to God. Therefore, I do not want you to lead this life of poverty any further. I want this girl to be brought up well and so I shall share with you a secret."

What was that secret?

"A rich man of Basra had made a vow that every night, he will bow down to me a hundred times and every Friday, he will do so *four hundred* times. But unfortunately, he failed to do so this last Friday. Now you must write a letter, in My name, and take it to him. The letter should state, "You have forgotten to bow down to me last Friday and so I want you to pay a penalty; and the penalty is that the person who has brought this letter to you should be given four hundred Dirhams."

When Rabiya's father woke up the next morning, he remembered the dream vividly. "I cannot understand what this dream means," he said to himself, "but I shall do as the voice instructed me."

He went to the rich man and handed over the letter to one of his servants. As soon as the rich man read the letter, he called for Rabiya's father, bowed down to him and said, "Whatever is written in this letter, is true. This Friday, my relatives visited me from a distant place, and so I forgot to pray and bow down to God four hundred times."

Then he requested Rabiya's father to tell him more about himself. Rabiya's father replied, "A baby girl has just taken birth in my house. We are so poor that we do not even have money to buy some oil to light a lamp."

On hearing this, the rich man was deeply moved. "God has asked me to give four hundred Dirhams, but I will give you one thousand Dirhams for the birth of this baby," he exclaimed. "At any time in the future, if you need anything, please do approach me without hesitation. It is because of this baby that God remembered me," he added.

And so Rabiya grew up. After a few years, her parents passed away, and Rabiya lived with her three sisters. Suddenly, their village faced a drought and the four sisters got separated from each other. Rabiya was still young at the time. A man spotted the orphan-girl. He thought to himself, "This girl is so beautiful! I shall kidnap her and sell her in the slave market. I am sure she will fetch a good price."

In those days there was a special market for the buying and selling of slaves. The man got hold of Rabiya and took her to the slave market. He sold Rabiya and received six Dirhams. Rabiya began to live and work as a slave at her new master's house.

Here, she was put through so many trials and troubles, that she decided to run away. She wished to go to a place where she could spend all her time in remembering God and repeating the Name Divine.

One night, when she saw everyone asleep, she realised that it was possible for her to escape. She ran away from there. She had just traversed a short distance when she fell into a ditch and broke her left hand.

Rabiya then said, "God, I ran away from my troubles to remember You, but what a situation You have put me into! I think the decision I made has not been in accordance with Your Will."

Then Rabiya heard a Divine voice, say to her, "Rabiya! I am the One who protects you. You need not do anything else, but just spend your life according to My Will."

Rabiya returned to her small room.

A few days passed. Then one night, Rabiya's master found that he could not sleep in peace. He was tossing and turning in bed; and he thought to himself that if he went for a short walk, he might be able to fall asleep later.

As he passed by Rabiya's room he saw a strange light shining from within. He was astonished. He wondered what this shining light could be. He opened the door and found Rabiya lost in deep prayer: "Give me love, give me deep longing for You, my Beloved. This is my plea, may I surrender my life unto You," she prayed. "God, My only desire is that I may surrender my entire self, whatever I am, whatever I have, to You! Though I have nothing, whatever little belongs to me, I surrender unto You, O Lord! God! My Master, for whom I am working, gives me food and shelter. So please shower Your generous blessings on him," she added.

When her Master heard these words, he realised that even though he had behaved so badly with her, the poor slave girl actually prayed for him!

Next morning he went to Rabiya and said to her, "I did not understand who you were. It was only last night that I realised that you are a great soul. Now I want to free you. But I wish that you continue to live here so that I may serve you."

"I am very grateful to you," Rabiya answered, "but now I shall leave from here because I want to spend my life in remembering God and surrendering to His Will".

Rabiya now left her master's house and went to live in another city. A person who went to meet her, described her thus: "She was sitting on the floor of mud in a small room which had just a bare mat and an earthen vessel filled with water. There was a bed made of wood, which she used to sit on to pray to God, and at night, to sleep. This was all her furniture."

One day Rabiya thought, "I wish I could travel to Mecca Sharif."

In those days, people had to travel from one place to another by foot. When Rabiya began her journey, a fellow pilgrim offered her a donkey to place her luggage on.

On the way, they had to pass through a forest and suddenly Rabiya's donkey collapsed. They asked Rabiya to give her luggage to them and continue the journey. But Rabiya refused their kind offer; she said she trusted the Lord who had brought her here, and He would definitely take care of her.

Suddenly, the donkey stirred and got up. Again Rabiya re-loaded the donkey with her luggage and walked on slowly and reached her destination. Her deep devotion and intense faith in God worked miracles for her in her daily life.

On one occasion, nine *dervishes* visited Rabiya. It was noon and Rabiya wished to offer some food to them. But, at that time, she had only two *rotis*. "How can I serve nine people with just two *rotis*?" she wondered. At that very moment a beggar passed by. He said, "I have been starving for three days. I beg you to give me something to eat in the Name of God." Rabiya gave both the *rotis* to him. She said, "It is a promise made by the Lord that whoever gives one in my Name, receives ten. Give one and get ten. My work is done. I have given 2 *rotis* in the Name of God, and I shall get twenty *rotis* in return."

A short while later an errand boy appeared from nowhere. He knocked at Rabiya's door and said, "My mistress has sent this basket of food for you." Rabiya asked the servant to open the basket. There were *rotis* and vegetables in it. She asked the servant to count the *rotis*. There were eighteen *rotis* in all. Rabiya said to the servant, "This basket of *rotis* is not meant for me. Please take it back."

"I asked God to send twenty *rotis*," she thought to herself. "He cannot just send eighteen *rotis*. Surely this basket is not for me." Just consider Rabiya's faith. The servant insisted, "How can I take this back? My mistress has sent it for you. Please tell me, why are you insisting that this food cannot be for you?"

Rabiya replied, "I have visitors at my place. I have to serve them food. Each visitor will eat at least two *rotis*. Thus, indeed, eighteen *rotis* for the visitors and one for me. I asked for one extra *roti*, in case anyone wanted more." On hearing this, the servant exclaimed, "My mistress had actually packed twenty *rotis*. But I was very hungry. I thought, Rabiya will surely not need twenty *rotis* as she is alone so I ate those two *rotis* on the way."

Rabiya was overwhelmed. With great fervor she called out, "O my Lord, You are great." Just then one of the *dervishes* said, "I am fasting today, so I will not eat anything." And now, Rabiya required only sixteen *rotis* for her guests and had in hand eighteen *rotis*. Once again the Lord had taken care of her need.

Rabiya was a great *sadhvi*, a true saint. Many people, who visited her, witnessed her state of poverty. She received marriage proposals from rich people. She would say, "I have already handed myself over to

God. If you want to marry me, then ask God for me. If God permits it, then I shall agree as I have completely surrendered myself at the Lotus Feet of God."

Rabiya was once seen surrounded by wild beasts who were watching her while she was praying. When *Dervish* Hassan came to see her, all the beasts ran away. When Rabiya opened her eyes, Hassan said to her, "Why did the beasts run away on seeing me?"

"What did you eat today?" Rabiya inquired of him. Hassan with a bent head replied: "Meat."

"Since you eat them up – how can they love you! They run for their life," Rabiya explained.

Rabiya's love moved out to all creation. She would always say, "A lover of God is one who is so lost in communion with God that he is unconscious of his own being and he cannot distinguish between pain and comfort."

Let us bow down before this great Mira of Islam and seek her blessings.

Sayings of Rabiya

"Lord! You know well that my keen desire is to carry out Your Commandments and to serve You with all my heart, O light of my eyes. If I were free, I would pass the whole day and night in prayers. But what should I do when You have made me the slave of a human being?"

* * * * *

"If I adore You out of fear of Hell, burn me in Hell!
If I adore You out of desire for Paradise,
Lock me out of Paradise.
But, if I adore You for Yourself alone,
Do not deny to me Your eternal beauty."

"I have loved Thee with two loves -
a selfish love and a love that is worthy of Thee.
As for the love which is selfish,
Therein I occupy myself with Thee,
to the exclusion of all others.
But in the love which is worthy of Thee,
Thou dost raise the veil that I may see Thee.
Yet is the praise not mine in this or that,
But the praise is to Thee in both that and this."

"Your hope in my heart is the rarest treasure
Your Name on my tongue is the sweetest word.
My choicest hours
Are the hours I spend with You –
O Allah, I can't live in this world
Without remembering You –
How can I endure the next world
Without seeing Your face?
I am a stranger in Your country
And lonely among Your worshippers:
This is the substance of my complaint."

"O God, take away the words of the devil
That mix with my prayer –
If not, then take my prayer as it is, devil and all."

Some Books by Rabiya

- *Doorkeeper of the Heart:* Versions of Rabi'a – by Rabi'a al-Adawiyya and Charles Upton
- *Perfume of the Desert* – Inspirations from Sufi Wisdom – Edited: A. Harvey and E. Hanut
- *Love Poems From God* – by Daniel Ladinsky

Some Books on Rabiya

- *Sufi Saints of East & West* – by Sadhu T.L. Vaswani
- *Women of Sufism: A Hidden Treasure* – by Camille Adams Helminski
- *First Among Sufis: The Life and Thought of Rabia al-Adawiyya, the Woman Saint of Basra* – by Widad El Sakkakini, Nabil Safwat and Doris Lessing
- *Rabia the Mystic:* A.D. *717-801* – by Margaret Smith
- *Rabi'a al-'Adawiyya, an 8th Century Islamic Saint from Iraq* – by Kathleen Jenks
- *Islamic Mysticism and Gender Identity* – by Leonard E. Hudson

Toyohiko Kagawa

Toyohiko Kagawa is remembered today as the Gandhi of Japan. Born to an affluent father, he gave up all worldly ambition to heed the call of Jesus. Rejecting the conventional life of a priest, he boldly went to live in a slum, to serve those who are ignored, neglected and condemned by society – the criminal, the harlot and the thief, as well as the poorest of the poor and the sick and afflicted. He lived among them, he fought for their rights, and he served as the conscience of a society which could not pretend that these unfortunate ones did not exist – at least, not while Kagawa was there to fight for them.

Toyohiko Kagawa

Let us reflect on the life of a great one: Toyohiko Kagawa, who was also called the Gandhi of Japan. Pacifist, labour activist and social reformer, Kagawa was also a great thinker who wrote over 150 highly acclaimed books, and actually went to live among the poorest of the poor in Japan, so that he could serve them.

Kagawa was born as the illegitimate son of a wealthy businessman in Kobe, Japan, on July 10, 1888. He did remarkably well at school. A brilliant career awaited the bright youngster. But, in the days of his youth and growing manhood, Kagawa was captivated by Jesus. At the age of twenty two, he gave up everything – wealth, position, power, and even his own good health to go and live in the slums and serve the slum dwellers.

Kagawa's extended family disowned him, when he embraced the Christian faith. But Kagawa was no blind convert; he was a firm believer in action. When he was enrolled in the Kobe Theological Seminary, he was disturbed and upset by the priests' obsession with matters of dogma and doctrine. For him, Christianity in action was the only truth. Arguing with the seminarians, he would cite to them repeatedly the Parable of the Good Samaritan. A devotee of Jesus Christ, he was also an ardent admirer of St. Francis, whose example he emulated, to become an apostle of brotherhood and love.

Kagawa was a born leader, a great organiser. His powerful impetus was behind several Movements in Japan, such as the Cooperative Movement, the Peasants' and Workers' Unions, as well as Consumer Societies. He took the initiative to set up small scale industries and cottage crafts to benefit the rural poor. He also helped to build dispensaries, hospitals and churches for disadvantaged people.

At that time, Japan was going through traumatic times, in the transition to capitalism. Those who suffered the most during this time of flux, were the common labourers. It was to serve them, help them and ameliorate their condition, that Kagawa decided to move into a slum – to live and move with the poorest of the poor, and be witness to their daily struggle. "I am a socialist because I am a Christian," he would often say.

He lived and worked and slept in cell-sized hovels, offering his love and compassion to criminals, gamblers and even murderers. He shared his life and all that he had, with those in need.

How did the people of the slum respond to this man of God? Many of them thought he was just an idealistic fool. Yet others exploited his goodness. Some of them did not hesitate to steal his money and clothes. Once, the very sheets on his bed were carried away by a neighbour. But Kagawa remained unperturbed, and continued to serve the slum dwellers with love.

A ruffian once knocked him down unconscious; Kagawa was left bleeding and bruised, with his front teeth broken. But his spirit of service was undaunted. Had not Jesus taught him to forgive his enemies, to turn the other cheek? Kagawa practised what Christ had preached. His special love and compassion was reserved for those whom society had discarded — drunkards, prostitutes and criminals. He did everything he could to help them. He even pawned his clothes to buy them food.

The slum in which he chose to live was Shinkawa — the worst area in Tokyo — a veritable hell in which over ten thousand people lived in conditions of utter deprivation. It was here that he chose to build his little hut, which he shared with beggars and destitutes.

There was a miserable man in Shinkawa, who suffered from terrible nightmares. The doctor told Kagawa that the only way to help him was to hold his hand at night, and comfort him whenever he felt disturbed. Kagawa kept awake, night after night, holding the wretched man's hand, until he was cured.

Sharing his hut with destitute and desperately ill people, he contracted trachoma, which led to loss of vision in one eye. This was not all. He bravely went to the aid of patients afflicted with TB – in those days, an incurable and a contagious disease. He nursed lepers. He cared for abandoned babies.

The doctors who treated him would often warn him, "You will not live long if you expose yourself to such risks." They were frightened when he actually contracted TB. But he himself was unmoved. "Lord, I shall spend each day that I have left, in Your service," he prayed.

And, indeed, his faith in God kept him going, against all odds. True to his prayer, he spent each day of his life in the service of God's suffering children. His sustained activism forced the government to rebuild slums and improve living conditions for the poorest of the poor. Kagawa continued to live amidst the slum dwellers, communing with Christ through service and sacrifice.

At one stage, he became so ill, that he had to shift out to a fishing village. It was feared that he would die. Here he wrote a book called *Across the Death Line*. The 'hero' of the book is a young man who is determined to serve the poor, despite ill-health, poverty and approaching death – Kagawa himself. He narrates a moving incident when he rushed to save the lives of men in an overturned boat. It was then that the cry awakened in his heart, "Let me not die! Let me live – but live for others!"

Kagawa's book became a bestseller. He was encouraged by his publisher to write more books – and his income grew to over fifty thousand dollars a year. With all this money, Kagawa was able to fund even more social service projects. He started six schools for educating workers; he began to publish a magazine called *The Soul of Freedom*.

Kagawa brought about significant changes in the life of the common man in Japan. He assisted in bringing universal adult male suffrage in 1925. Following this, he fought for women's suffrage and campaigned for a peaceful foreign policy. In 1928, he successfully organised the Japanese Federation of Labour, as well as the National Anti War League. He was thrown in prison repeatedly, for his anti-establishment activities.

At this time, a massive earthquake struck Japan. Millions of people were affected; tens of thousands of homes and businesses were destroyed; famine, disease and anarchy followed one another. The government struggled to organise relief and rehabilitation for the people. The authorities realised that there was one man who could coordinate relief operations speedily and efficiently – and he was in jail at that time! By a special order, the government released him from the prison and requested him to organise relief measures.

The people were thrilled to see him out of prison. They gave him a hero's welcome. The government hastened to offer him a plush office, a large salary, a chauffeured car and other perks befitting a high official. Kagawa turned down their flattering offer: "I shall definitely take up the administration of relief operations," he said. "But I shall accept no salary to serve my brothers and sisters."

To say that the authorities were stunned would be an understatement. "But why should you not accept these facilities?" they persisted. "You will be working for the government."

"To work with the poor," Kagawa said to them, "I must be poor."

The entire government machinery was at his disposal, but he organised a band of eighty student volunteers, and went about the task of relief and reconstruction, speedily and efficiently.

They called him Kagawa the fearless; what made him fearless was his tremendous love and sympathy for the poor.

He was a simple soul; he loved the simple life. He was at home amidst trees and flowers and flowing brooks. "When I am close to nature, when I hear the birds, owls and rabbits call, I feel happy to be alive," he said.

Kagawa lived and worked for the poor, in whom he beheld Jesus Christ. For him, the Cross symbolised the power of Christ's love, and the power of suffering for the sake of what is righteous and true. This was why he chose to live and work in Japan's worst slums, among the people whom he sought to serve. He was dismissive of what he called 'pulpit' religion; what he believed in and practised all his life, was the religion of love-in-action.

Towards the end of his life, he lay in a hospital, threatened with total blindness.

"Aren't you afraid of losing your sight?" his friends asked him. "Aren't you afraid of approaching death?"

"There's nothing to fear in this wide, wonderful, God-filled world," was his calm reply.

"As I lie in this dark room," he said, "God still radiates light. The pains that pierce my body are like the very flames of hell – but even in these melting fires, I feel God's love enfolding me!"

Kagawa passed away in the year 1960. The Emperor conferred Japan's highest honour upon him posthumously – The Order of The Sacred Treasure. On his 1st Death Anniversary, over a hundred friends and admirers – professors, workers, students, patients, writers and others – brought out a two-volume biography of Kagawa, each one of them contributing an essay as his/her personal tribute.

Kagawa's message was simple: God dwells among the poorest of the poor; to feed them, clothe them, serve them and love them, is equivalent to serving God. Truly, he beheld Jesus among the poor, the miserable, the downtrodden and the sick. In fellowship with them, he felt himself in fellowship with God.

Homage to this great mystic!

Sayings of Kagawa

"Whosoever will be great among you...shall be the servant of all. Only by service to others can a man, or nation, be Godlike."

* * * * *

"Communism's only power is to diagnose some of the ills of disordered society. It has no cure. It creates only an infantile paralysis of the social order."

* * * * *

"Love is creation raised to a higher degree."

* * * * *

"God knows the secret plan of the things He will do for the world, using my hand."

* * * * *

"The darkness is a holy of holies of which no one can rob me. In the darkness I meet God face to face."

* * * * *

"Not everything in man's life is summed up in the problem of food. Anyone who thinks that a civilisation can be founded on bread alone makes a great mistake. No matter how much bread there is, it cannot produce a man: it can only nourish him. Life exists before food. Man's life comes from the very origin of life. Therefore civilisation does not follow the forms of production. All social life follows the action of life."

* * * * *

"Love is the ultimate revelation, the final sanctuary."

* * * * *

"The definition of religion has been rewritten by Jesus. It is not merely a question of man relying on God; it is also of God coming down to earth and experiencing man's way of living..."

* * * * *

"O God, make me like Your Christ!"

* * * * *

"God is love! God is love! Where love is, there is God."

Some Books by Toyohiko Kagawa

- *Meditations on The Cross* – by Toyohiko Kagawa, Helen F. Topping, and Marion R. Draper
- *Living Out Christ's Love*
- *Kagawa: Songs From the Slums*
- *The Willow and the Bridge: Poems and Meditations* – by Toyohiko Kagawa and Franklin Cole
- *Brotherhood Economics*
- *Love, the Law of Life*
- *A Grain of Wheat*
- *Songs From the Land of Dawn* – by Lois Johnson Erickson, Toyohiko Kagawa
- *Meditations*
- *Behold the Man* – by Toyohiko Kagawa, Maxine Shore, Milo Milton Oblinger
- *Christ and Japan*
- *New Life Through God*
- *Across The Death Line*

Some Books on Kagawa

- *A seed shall serve: the story of Toyohiko Kagawa: Spiritual leader of modern Japan* – by Charlie May Hogue Simon
- *Saint in the Slums. The Story of Kagawa of Japan* – by Cyril Davey
- *Toyohiko Kagawa: An Apostle of Love and Social Justice* – by Robert D. Schildgen
- *Kagawa: An Apostle of Japan* – by Margaret Baumann
- *Kagawa, Gambler for God* – by Allan A. Hunter
- *Kagawa* – by William Axling

Jamshed Nusserwanji

Jamshed Nusserwanji was one of the great sons of undivided India. For him, to live was to love, to serve, to share the bounties of life, to bear the burdens of others. He was a burden-bearer and a peacemaker. A Parsi by birth, he loved the Gita as much as he did the Zend Avesta. He was a mayor who made Karachi one of the cleanest cities in undivided India. He was a *karma-yogi* who taught that God is Love and the way to God is the way of truth and compassion.

Jamshed Nusserwanji

There is a story of a man who was about to enter heaven.

He is still at the gates of heaven when he hears a voice calling out to him. It comes from a remote corner of the earth. It says, "I am in great agony; is there no one to help?" And the man who is about to enter paradise, says to himself, "Not for me the joys of the heaven-world, for someone is suffering on earth. Back to the earth I go!"

Such a man was Jamshed Nusserwanji.

He was born in a wealthy family. He spent all his riches and became poor for the sake of the poor whom he loved dearly. They came to him in endless rows: he refused none. He gave something to everyone who came to him. None returned, empty-handed, from his door. To some he gave money: to some he gave clothes: to some he gave food: and to all he gave the benedictions of his loving heart.

One day, a friend came to him, and said, "On my way to meet you, I came across a poor widow, and her children; they were being thrown out of their house with all their belongings, because the house had been mortgaged by her husband, and the widow was unable to redeem it."

"What is the amount of the mortgage?" Jamshed asked.

"Five thousand rupees," was the answer.

What did Jamshed Nusserwanji do? Quietly, he went to his inner apartment and brought out the required amount, handed it over to the friend and asked him to have the mortgage redeemed. Jamshed did not even care to enquire who the widow was. To him one human being in need was as good as any other.

He often said to himself, "What I hoard, I lose. What I scatter, I save." His heart was wide as an ocean. And he became a helper of every good cause. He helped individuals and institutions. Schools and colleges, asylums and orphanages, hospitals and homes of mercy received freely of his benevolence.

He was elected and re-elected as the Mayor of Karachi for 9 terms. I refer, of course, to the period before Independence when Karachi was a part of undivided India. The city's cleanliness, hygiene and sanitation spoke volumes of the quality of his work. He was also responsible for the scientific planning and layout of streets, water-supply, and several other good things in the city.

Born amidst wealth and comfort, he learnt to renounce luxury, to live on simple food. Though, he could afford to live in a large palatial building, he actually lived in a tiny room which served as an all-in-one study, bed-room and sitting room. He slept on a simple wooden board. He never lost his temper and always had a smile on his face and a pleasing countenance.

Jamshed usually awoke in the dark of the dawn and spent the early hours of the day in silent meditation.

He worked throughout the day. He met people, looked into their needs, listened to their problems, and gave them his advice. It is said he worked for sixteen hours a day. And yet, his face was ever fresh and radiant.

There were occasions when people, whom he had helped greatly, spoke ill of him, maligned him, spread wrong reports against his saintly character. In return he blessed them. Whenever they came to him, in times of need, he did not withhold his helping hand. His love moved out to all, irrespective of their race, religion or creed.

Jamshed loved the leper and the outcast. He was young in years when this love first welled up within his heart. One day, as he returned with his friends, from the market-place, a leper, with horrible sores all over, came to him and begged for alms. His friends, repulsed by the sight, shrank away. But Jamshed moved forward and embraced the leper: tears trickled down the cheeks of both. The leper had never known what it was to be loved. Compassion for lepers, grew in the heart of Jamshed, as the years passed. It is said that towards the close of his life, he expressed a desire to go and live in the midst of lepers in the Hiranand Leper Asylum at Mangho Pir, Karachi. "They have shelter and food and receive medical treatment," he said. "But their hearts are hungry for love. They need companionship, I want to go and live in their midst, and share with them the love of my heart. It will mean, I know, complete severance from my friends and relatives, from everything that is dear to me now. It may also mean that, one day, I too, may become a leper. But the body has to go any how: why must it not go while serving the neglected ones and the outcast?"

He was a man of prayer. And to all who looked to him for guidance, he said, "Build your life in prayer. And, remember, whenever you are in trouble, call out to God and He will come to your rescue!"

There is an amazing incident from his life which illustrates the power of true faith and prayer. One afternoon, Jamshed was in his car, and he asked the driver to take him to a particular place. When the car stopped, Jamshed realised that he had been brought to the wrong place. Instead of getting annoyed, he took it as God's Will, and got down from the car to visit the house of a friend who lived in that locality. As he reached the house and opened the door, he heard the troubled cries of a young woman. "Jamshed! Jamshed! Where is your God? Why does he not come to my rescue?" The young woman was trying to escape through a window from the clutches of a voluptuous man who had broken into her house to violate her chastity. Quickly Jamshed entered the room and said, "My dear, He is here!" To many, indeed, Jamshed was a God. His faith in God was strong and unshakeable. He lived up to the ideals of simplicity, service, and compassion.

His earthly voyage came to an end when he was 66. An Englishman – a Buddhist by faith – who met Jamshed, said of him, "I met the greatest man. He radiated an aura of peace and inner enlightenment. If ever a man was Christ-like, it was he."

His life is an inspiration to many of us. May it continue to be an inspiration to generations unborn!

Sayings of Jamshed Nusserwanji

"I pray daily to God:
God, make me useful,
God, keep me harmless,
God, Keep me pure,
God, make me Your channel.
This is all I pray."

Some Books on Jamshed Nusserwanji

- *Jamshed Nusserwanji: A prophet of the poor* (East and West series) – by Sadhu Vaswani
- *Jamshed Nusserwanji Mehta - A Life Sketch* – by World Zoroastrian Organization
- *Of Parsi philanthropy* – Sunnu Farrokh Golwalla

Ibrahim Ibn Adham

Ibrahim was a saint who paid a great price for poverty. In truth, he gave up his kingdom and his life of comfort, luxury and power to lead the life of a *fakir*, in search of the Truth. Living a life of austerity, self denial and dedication to the Lord, he conquered the lower self of the ego, to become one of the greatest Sufi saints of all times.

Ibrahim Ibn Adham

"As you think, so you become." This is a great law. If you meditate on holy men, you will become more and more like them. This is why, our ancestors urged us to listen to or read about the lives of the holy ones of humanity.

The saint of whom I am about to tell you, was a king – the King of Balkh. He lived in a mansion and was surrounded by luxury. He had but to lift a finger, and several servants would come running to attend to his command.

Everyday, a cart load of fresh flowers would be brought to his palace. All these flowers would be spread on the king's bed. I mention this only to tell you that he lived a life of unbelievable luxury.

One day, while he was sitting in his court (*darbar*), a man walked in, pulled out his cotton bedspread and said, "I am looking for a little space, where I can relax."

The king was astonished! Interrupting the stranger he said, "This is not a *caravanserai*, this is my court!"

"Pardon me," said the stranger, "Can I place a few questions before you?"

The king told him to proceed.

The stranger began his questions. "Today, you reside in this mansion, but do you know who lived here before you?"

The king answered, "Before me, my father resided here. He was the king of this land and his name was Adham!"

The stranger continued. "Where is your father now?"

The king replied, "My father is no more."

The stranger went on, "Before your father, there must have been somebody else who lived here."

The king answered, "Yes, my grandfather resided here." The stranger once again probed, "So where is he now?" The king replied in the same manner, "He is no more with us in this world."

Yet again the stranger queried, "Who lived here before him?" The king retorted with a similar answer.

Then it was that the stranger says to the king, "What would you call a place where one stays for a short time and leaves? You call it a traveller's inn, a *caravanserai*. People come here, live here for some days and then they leave. O dear king, you too, must regard your palace as a traveller's inn, as one day, you too, will have to leave this place."

Having uttered these words, the stranger rolls up his bedding in a bundle and hoists it on his shoulders, and vanishes as quickly, as he had come.

The stranger may have left, but each and every word that he had spoken, kept echoing and reverberating in the king's mind.

"This world is nothing but a traveller's inn, a resting place. No one will live here forever."

The words haunted the king. Many times, he would sit silently in a corner and cogitate, questioning. "Why have I come upon this earth?" He would constantly reflect on the purpose of life.

One day, the king went out hunting, accompanied by his courtiers.

He saw a beautiful deer from a distance. He started chasing the deer, and in his pursuit, he was separated from his retinue.

Very soon the king found himself alone in the wilderness. Then he heard a Voice. It said to him, "Ibrahim, arise, awake, before death swallows thee!"

The words were repeated several times. On hearing them, the king fell down in a swoon.

When he recovered, he saw the deer standing close to him. He immediately aimed his arrow at the animal. But, before he could shoot the arrow, the deer began to speak to him: "I have come to hunt you, not to be hunted down by you! You cannot harm me. Has God created you only to kill and destroy lives?"

The king was wonderstruck.

Other similar experiences followed this incident.

One day, the king had a dream. In that dream, he heard the continuous noise of people's footsteps coming and going on his terrace. The king wondered who the people were on the terrace. He decided to go and check for himself. Climbing on to the terrace, he found people hurriedly walking to and fro. Perplexed, he asked them, "What are all of you doing? Why are you here on my terrace? What is it that you seek?"

The people immediately responded, "We have lost our camels! We are looking for them here."

The king laughed uproariously, "You are all fools," he said. "You say you have lost your camels, and are looking for them here on the terrace?" The people also laugh and say to him, "We are just as foolish as you are! You don the robes of a king, and hope to find God in this mansion. Even so, we search for our camels on this terrace!"

In the morning, when the king woke up, he recollected the dream, and his life was transformed. He renounced his power and wealth. He left behind all his treasures; he gave up his silk robes and donned simple clothes. He then walked out of the palace in search of the Lord. He visited many places, and finally came to Nishapur. He planned to reside in the woods near Nishapur. He began to live in a cave. Out of seven days in a week, he would meditate for six days. On the seventh day, Sunday, he would go to the forest and chop some wood. He would sell the chopped wood and whatever money he made from it, he shared with other ascetics who stayed in the caves and from the remaining, he bought *rotis* which sufficed as his meals for the rest of the week. Initially, the *rotis* would be fresh, but with time, they would get stale and hard. Then he would dip them in water to make them soft and edible. He underwent a lot of hardships and made many sacrifices. He never combed his hair, which remained matted.

Sometimes, when he would get hungry, and had nothing to eat, he would chew on a piece of stick. The stick on which he used to chew, has the marks of his teeth on it and is still preserved in his *Dargah*.

In Sufi literature, there is a word which has been used repeatedly. The word is *nafs*. *Nafs* means the lower self; it means the ego self, the lower self of passion and pride, of lust and hatred, of envy and jealousy, of ill will and greed.

The king lived a life of denial and dedication, in order to conquer this *nafs*.

For forty years, the king walked without any shoes. He roamed around, with no care for his comfort. Then suddenly, the grace of Allah poured on him. He now knew the Truth that he had sought all these years. Devotees started getting drawn to him. The fame of Ibrahim spread.

One day, a poor man, who had no food to eat and no clothes to wear, was cursing God. Ibrahim heard him and said to him, "My dear, you have received this life of poverty free, and so you have no value for it."

Surprised, the beggar asked him, "Does one have to pay for poverty!"

The king said, "Yes, I have purchased it. I renounced my kingdom, my wealth and everything I had. Hence I know the value of poverty. I believe that being poor, is one of the richest blessings of life."

One day, a rich man brought to him a thousand rupees and asked him to accept the money. Ibrahim *Darvesh* looked at this man and said to him, "I don't accept money from people who are poorer than me." Astounded, the rich person said, "I am not a poor person. Look at me. I am a rich man. I have everything."

Hearing this Ibrahim said, "Do you desire to accomplish and acquire more?" The rich man immediately said, "Yes indeed! I do."

Ibrahim said, "How can a person who desires more, be called rich? And, so how can I accept money from a person who is poor?"

Once, Ibrahim had a desire to visit Mecca. A caravan was heading towards Mecca, and he decided to join this caravan. In the meantime, at Mecca, people heard that Ibrahim, formerly, the King of Balkh and Bukhara, the one who had renounced everything and embraced poverty, was heading towards Mecca. People began to gather together to meet him and welcome him to the holy city.

When Ibrahim came to know of this, he slipped away from the caravan. He arrived at Mecca ahead of the caravan. People saw that the caravan had arrived and gathered together. Ibrahim joined them and stood there, in the crowd. The people asked him, "Do you know anything about the caravan? Is Ibrahim coming in it?"

Look at the amazing reply Ibrahim *Darvesh* gives them; "Ibrahim! You talk and ask about Ibrahim! That person who is a thief, a cheat?" The people immediately surround him and start beating him up, "How can you talk like this about such a noble soul, such a *fakir* of the Lord? You yourself are a liar, a thief, and a cheat!!!"

To that Ibrahim said, "That is exactly what I am saying." People did not understand what he said and they continued to hit him.

A passerby looked at his face. He recognised him and said, "Are you Ibrahim?" Ibrahim replied, "Yes, people do call me by this name." The person asked, "Are you Ibrahim Ibn Adham?" Ibrahim nodded his head in agreement.

"Were you the King of the Balkh and Bukhara?" the person asked again. "Yes, indeed I was once upon a time, the King of the Balkh and Bukhara."

The man then reminded the king, "I was your *vazir*, your minister. Perhaps you don't remember me. I could not place you initially either. But, now when I see your eyes, they are the eyes of my King. I remember that your eyes were blue. But, what is this? Why have you been reduced to this poor state? Please, come and visit the palace. Your son is now the king. He will be overjoyed to see you. He will readily hand you back your kingdom."

Ibrahim was holding a needle and a thread in his hand; he dropped the needle in the river and said to the *vazir*, "Before I give you the answer to your question, please bring back the needle that I dropped into the river."

The minister said in astonishment, "The needle you dropped in the river? How can I bring it back? If you are in need of another needle, I can get one for you." Ibrahim *Darvesh* replied, "No I don't need any other needle but the one that I dropped in the river. If you cannot bring the needle back, then wait." And he shut his eyes and prayed. A few minutes later, a fish emerged out of the river and brought back the needle. Ibrahim *Darvesh* took the needle from the fish's mouth and told the minister, "Once, I was the King of the Balkh and Bukhara. But, now I am the King of the whole universe. All the three worlds are under my control: whatever I need, I get from Allah. What is there that Allah cannot give!"

Ibrahim urged people to take the path of total surrender. He narrated a story to explain total surrender.

Once, I purchased a slave. I asked him, "By what name shall I call you?"

"I shall accept any name by which you call me," was his spontaneous reply.

I asked him, "What would you like to eat?"

"That which you will give me," he replied again.

"What garments would you like to wear," I further asked.

"The ones that you, in your kindness, will bestow on me," he replied.

"What tasks would you perform," I inquired.

"That which you assign me," he replied.

"What is your desire," I questioned.

"I am but a slave, how can I have a separate will?" he said.

Then it is that I said to myself, "I wish, I was a slave of Allah and had surrendered totally to Him, as this slave had done to His Master."

Ibrahim used to say again and again, to his disciples, "Open up that which you have kept tied; and tie up that which you have left open."

What is it that we have kept tied? We keep our purses tied. Open up your purses and share the wealth you have with the poor and the needy. Learn to tie up that which is open. What is open? Our tongues! Therefore, talk less!

All the Sufi saints stress on this one point, that one must speak little. If you wish to speak, then speak only about God and his holy men. Speak as much you like to God. There are no limits to that. But if you wish to discuss worldly and materialistic things, then seal up your tongue.

Open what is closed and close that which is open!

One day, Ibrahim came across a soldier who enquired about the way to the city. In reply, Ibrahim pointed in the direction of the graveyard. Irritated, the soldier hit Ibrahim on the head causing a serious wound. He then tied him up with a rope and dragged him to the city. People recognised Ibrahim and pointed out to the soldier the blunder he had committed. The soldier retaliated, "But he showed me the wrong way." Ibrahim calmly explained to him that a town is where the population decreases everyday, while that of the graveyard is everyday increasing. Is not the graveyard then really a developing town? The soldier recognised the saint and fell at his feet.

Dear friends, when the call comes, at the moment of death, we leave everything behind. So all that we have amassed is useless, for we are unable to take it along with us on the final journey. Only one thing survives through this journey, and that is love. It is the only thing that we can carry with ourselves. Therefore, nurture love in your hearts - nourish it and share it with others.

The teachings of God are summed up in these few points. Untie the tied and tie the untied. Revere the world and love God and surrender yourself totally to him!

Sayings of Ibrahim Ibn Adham

"To become a saint of God, you must covet nothing in this world or the next and you must give yourself entirely to God and turn your face to Him. To desire this world is turning away from God for the sake of what is transitory. To covet the next world means turning away from God for the sake of what is everlasting."

* * * * *

"Faith in God will be firmly established if three veils are cast aside:
1. Feeling pleasure in possessing anything.
2. Lamenting over the loss of anything.
3. Enjoying self-praise."

* * * * *

"Say not 'tomorrow' or the 'day after tomorrow'; for those that perished, perished because they lived always in their hopes, until the truth came upon them suddenly in their heedlessness."

* * * * *

"Anyone who controls his stomach is in control of his religion, and anyone who controls his hunger is in control of good behaviour. Disobedience towards Allah is nearest to a person who is satiated with a full stomach, and furthest away from a person who is hungry."

* * * * *

"He who wishes that people always remember him with goodness is neither God-fearing nor sincere."

* * * * *

"The Sufi is free from all attachments to material goods and also free from influences of the desires; he/she is therefore poor, possessing nothing and letting nothing possess him/her."

Some Books on Ibrahim Ibn Adham

- *Sufi Saints of East & West* – by Sadhu T.L. Vaswani
- *Hikayat Sultan Ibrahim Ibn Adham: An Edition of an Anonymous Malay Text* (Monograph Series, No 27) – by Russell Jones
- *The Concise Encyclopaedia of Islam* – by Cyril Glasse and Huston Smith

Latif Shah

Few of us have heard of **Latif Shah**, the Muslim saint from Maharashtra, who was an ardent devotee of Sri Krishna. Latif Shah was a symbol of deep devotion and yearning for the Lord. What cannot such devotion achieve? The Lord enacted a divine *leela* – He performed a miracle, to protect His devotee, at a critical juncture in his life. Latif Shah knew the secret of eternal freedom, utter surrender to the Lord.

Latif Shah

For centuries, through the magnetism of his pure love, Sri Krishna has attracted many souls towards Him.

Krishna is He who attracts!

We are told that Sri Krishna incarnated Himself 5,000 years ago and appeared on this earth plane. But even today, He continues to draw people towards Himself.

Not only Hindus, but also people of other faiths, such as Christians and Muslims, have felt drawn to Him.

May I tell you of a Muslim devotee of Sri Krishna? He was born in the 16th century in Maharashtra. His name was Latif Shah. A great poet-saint of Sind, Pakistan, also had the name Shah Latif. But this lover of Sri Krishna was named Latif Shah.

Even though he was born in a Muslim family, there arose in his heart from childhood, a deep devotion for Lord Krishna. When he heard the name of Sri Krishna for the first time, an electric current seemed to pass through his entire body. He began to ask people about Sri Krishna. He wanted to know more and more about the Lord. As he heard about Sri Krishna's *leelas*, the devotion in his heart increased manifold.

He began to study the Srimad Bhagavad Gita and the Bhagavad Purana. Whenever he read the Bhagavad Purana, tears would roll down from his eyes.

Many of us read the Bhagavad Purana, at one time or another; but how many of us have such devotion? Whenever Latif Shah uttered the Name of Krishna or read about Him, tears would gush forth from his eyes. Whenever he read the Bhagavad Gita aloud, people would stop to listen to *slokas* of the Gita being sung in his melodious voice.

In those days, Latif Shah lived in a part of the India which was under a Muslim ruler. People went to this ruler and complained against the devout man. "Latif Shah is a Muslim, yet he openly reads the Bhagavad Gita and the Bhagavad Purana," they said to the ruler. "How can you allow this to go on?" When the Muslim ruler heard this, he was wild with rage. He ordered the soldiers to bring Latif Shah to his presence. He thought, "Once Latif Shah comes here, I shall send some soldiers to pull his house down, so that he will have no place to stay in. That will surely teach him a lesson!"

The soldiers, on hearing the orders of the king, rushed to bring Latif Shah. The king waited impatiently for Latif Shah to come. Minutes passed by, hours passed by, neither the soldiers nor Latif Shah arrived at the court. The king lost his patience. He said, "I will wait no longer, I will mount a horse and go to Latif Shah's house to see what is happening."

It so happened that when the soldiers reached Latif Shah's house, he was singing the Bhagavad Purana in his mellifluous voice. When the soldiers heard his song, they forgot everything. There were many devotees sitting around Latif Shah and the soldiers also sat down with them. In their hearts, they felt intense joy and peace. They had never experienced such bliss before. They said to themselves, "What a pity, we did not come here earlier to receive and experience this joy!"

After some time, the king arrived, red hot with anger. He saw his soldiers sitting with other devotees in a *satsang*, while Latif Shah read from the great scripture, *Srimad Bhagavad*. Behind Latif Shah, was a very beautiful picture of Sri Krishna and Radharani. In Radha's hand there was a *paan*, or betel leaf. The picture depicted Radha trying to feed the *paan* to Sri Krishna.

Once, a little girl told me, "Today is my birthday, and I have eaten a *paan* worth Rs 100." Just imagine, one *paan* for Rs 100! When I was a little boy, we used to get a *paan* for one *paisa*. As you know, *paan* is very tasty. There is betel nut in them, crushed coconut and *gulkand* (sweet rose crush). And the little girl was so happy that she had eaten a *paan* worth Rs 100. I do not know which type of *paan* was in Radha's hand. But Radha wanted to feed the *paan* to her Beloved Lord, Sri Krishna.

When the king saw the picture of Sri Krishna and Radharani, he said to Latif Shah in a mocking tone, "You are reading the Bhagavad, you are making up useless stories about your Krishna. But does your Krishna hear you? Look at this picture. For years Lord Krishna and Radha have been standing here. Till now, poor Radha has not been able to feed the *paan* to Lord Krishna. And yet you keep repeating Krishna, Krishna. Where is your Krishna?"

Let me stress this – this is a true incident recorded in history. It happened in the 16th century. When Latif Shah heard the king, he stood up, joined his hands and pleaded with Sri Krishna, "O Krishna, what is there that You cannot do? Please part Your lips, so that Radha can feed the *paan* to You."

At that very moment a miracle came to pass. All the people seated there, as also the king, witnessed that Lord Krishna in the picture, opened His mouth and Radha fed Him the *paan*. When the king saw this miracle, he fell at the feet of Latif Shah and begged for forgiveness. He said to the saint, "Latif Shah, I was going to break down your house. I was not aware that you are a true devotee of God. Please forgive me, and bestow on me your blessings and grace."

Latif Shah has composed many songs in the Marathi language, which are still devoutly sung in some

Maharashtrian homes. In these holy songs, he praises greatly, the grace of the guru. In his songs, one thing is emphasised: that it is only when there is deep thirst in the heart of the devotee that the Lord appears: only when we call out to Sri Krishna with love, longing and deep yearning of the heart, only then is the devotee capable of treading the path of *bhakti*.

In his *bhajans* and songs, Latif Shah urged the people to cultivate love and longing in their hearts, an intense thirst for the Beloved. In one of his songs, he says, "This world is falsehood, it is a mirage. This world is a net and we are ensnared in it. The things we are running after are mere reflections and illusions. They have no substance. Alas! we realise this truth only when the last moment arrives! Nothing that we accumulate, can be carried beyond this earth. Everything is mortal, perishable, ephemeral. Alas, we have not collected that which is immortal and have not gathered the treasure for which we were sent to this earth plane."

I was at a rural retreat sometime ago. There were flowing waters and a small pond had been formed. Some fishermen were fishing there and every time they caught a fish, it struggled for life, gasping for breath. At that time, there was a kind gentleman who was standing by my side. He felt a deep sense of compassion for the fish. He told the fishermen, "Give me all the fish; in exchange you may take as much money as you wish from me." The fishermen gave him all the fish. The gentleman put the fish back into the pond. At that time it occurred to me, "We too are like these fishes. We too, are trapped in the net of falsehood. We can be released from that net, only if someone is ready to purchase us and pay the price. Who will pay the price to release us? Only a saint or a guru can do that for us."

This world is a facade, an illusion. Gold, silver and money are all dust.

Latif Shah asks in his songs, "What can the unfortunate people do? They are prisoners, prisoners of their cravings and desires." There are desires within each and every one of us. And desires make us dance to their tune. We commit so many sins because of these desires. We are frittering away our lives after these futile wants and desires, and in their pursuit, alas, we waste our invaluable breaths.

Latif Shah says, "Without the mercy and grace of a saint or guru, you cannot attain immortality. That is why, we should surrender ourselves to a guru. We can be extricated from the prison of this world only through His grace."

Blessed be his name!

Ma Saradamani

Ma **Saradamani** was the *Sangha-mata,* the head of the Ramakrishna Order for over thirty years and she carried out her duty with dignity, sweetness and strength. The most dominant quality of her life was her motherly love. Rightly is she revered by thousands all over the world as the Holy Mother. She may have been uneducated, but she was an illumined soul. Her life bears witness to the truth that *moksha* or salvation is as open to ordinary housewives as it is to those who renounce the world and dedicate themselves to a ceaseless search of God. She will continue to be a source of strength and inspiration to generations unborn.

Ma Saradamani

I am sometimes asked this question, specially by women: why is it that while there have appeared many male saints, very few women are revered as saints? Why is that so?

There was a time when every woman was a saint, hence the name of so many saints could not be mentioned. Each woman was a saint – for each woman's life was pure and holy. Each woman's life was filled with devotion, with longing for the Lotus Feet of the Lord. Each woman was aware of the purpose of this human birth and did her best to achieve it.

The men were different. Hence when a few of them became saints, we remember them. But there were so many saints among women, that mentioning all of them would need encyclopedias.

Let us reflect on the life of a woman-saint, Ma Saradamani. She was born on December 22, 1853, in a small village of Bengal, called Jairamabati. She was born in a poor family and was the eldest child. She had six younger brothers and sisters. From childhood

Saradamani had a tremendous affinity for God. She had little interest in games commonly played by children. Her friends would invite her to come and play with them. But Sarada's attention was focused on the idols of God. She would say, these idols are my dolls. She would decorate the idols with flowers and sacred leaves. Since her childhood, she was filled with deep affection and the spirit of caring. If ever she saw any child crying, she would try to carry him in her lap. She would hug the child, give him love and speak sweet words to him. Little children regarded her as their second mother. She had tremendous love too, for birds and animals.

One day, she found a calf writhing in pain. She stayed up all night to take care of the calf. She rubbed his stomach gently throughout the night and prayed to God to heal the calf. You can pass on this stomach ache to me, she implored God. But please let this poor calf not bear this pain any more.

There was a cuckoo who would look at Sarada and cry out 'Maa, Maa, Maa'. Hearing this, the villagers would laugh. There was a stray cat, whom the villagers would try to shoo away. But Saradamani would pour her love even onto that cat. With her own hands she would give it milk to drink. Since childhood she had a tender heart filled with love and the spirit of caring.

She had a strong desire to study. But in those days girls were not encouraged to go to school. Sarada would go to leave her younger brother at school and would not return back. She would stay back in school and would learn to read and write. She could read the holy scriptures. She would also watch religious dramas and listen to stories from the Indian epics.

At the age of five, she was wedded to Sri Ramakrishna Parmahansa who was then called Gadhadhar. He had the job of a priest at the Dakshineshwar temple. After two years Gadhadhar visited his birth place, Kamarpurkar. When he returned to Dakshineshwar, divine longing seized him. The thought that constantly arose in his mind was, "People come walking for miles, just to have a glimpse of Ma Kali's statue. Is this merely a statue or is there some power in it, a power which attracts and draws people? If the Mother has an existence, why does she not reveal herself to me?"

Often, while calling out to Her, he would start weeping. Many a times while sobbing, he would lose his consciousness. People thought that he was seized by a disease. News even travelled to Kamarpurkar that Gadhadhar had gone mad. Once, while he was sitting in the temple, he even lifted the sword that was in Kali Ma's hand and challenged, "Ma, if you do not appear before me, I will kill myself."

All this while, Saradamani had been living apart from him. Now there arose within her the desire to meet her husband.

One day she came to know that Ramakrishna had come to Kamarpurkar for a few days. Sarada went to meet him. Ramakrishna met her with great affection. "Sarada", he said to her, "why did you take so long in coming to me?" On hearing those words, Sarada's heart was filled with joy. Her husband said to her, "Sarada, do not forget even for a moment the purpose for which the human birth has been given to you. We have been given this priceless birth to become one with our Lord, our Beloved. Hence, create within you a thirst for the Lord and envision the form of Lord in each one. Serve them. If you have to live in the world, then fulfill the duties of the world. But while living in the world, do not become worldly. Do not get enmeshed in the world, do not get attached to anybody or anything."

Sarada now felt the pull to go to her husband. Some women of the village were going to Kolkata for a bath in the Ganga. Sarada joined the pilgrim band. They walked continuously for three to four days. Sarada was tired and could not walk further. She came down with malarial fever accompanied by shivering. The temperature soared high. It became impossible for her to walk in spite of her deep desire to continue the journey.

That night, she saw, in her dream, a vision of a girl with dark complexion, but exquisitely beautiful, who came and nursed and caressed her. There was a soothing coolness in her hand. As she caressed Sarada, her temperature went on reducing. Sarada asked her, "Ma, who are You?" She replied, "I am your sister. I have come to receive you."

Sarada carried on her journey and reached Dakshineshwar. Ramakrishna greeted her with great love and affection. He himself took care of her. Within three-four days she recovered fully.

Now Saradamani stayed in a room on the ground floor of the temple. The room was about fifty feet long and the ceiling only nine feet high. There was no window to that room. There were only two ventilators (or skylights) and a four foot high door. One had to bend low to enter the room. It seemed as though the room was teaching each one who entered to be humble.

Sarada would meet her husband for a short while at night and take his blessings. She would be up by 3 am or 4 am, when the rest of the world slept. She would go to the river Ganga for her bath. Then she spent time in prayer and meditation. This was followed by cooking meals for her husband. She would keep herself busy all the time.

Sri Ramakrishna's mercy and blessings on Sarada were so bountiful that he accepted her as his disciple – and yet worshiped her as the Universal Mother. They lived a pure life, devoid of physical contact. Indeed, their marriage was truly the union of two souls. Instead of dragging one another down to the worldly level, they elevated themselves to the level of the Divine.

In June 1885, Sri Ramakrishna came down with throat cancer. Saradamani served him ceaselessly. On

August 15, 1988, Sri Ramakrishna gave up his physical body. Saradamani said to herself, "Now I am a widow. How can I wear bangles?" She decided to remove them. But she had worn them when she had got married at the age of five. Now, as an adult, her wrist had widened and the bangles would not come off. She took a hammer and was about to break them, when she suddenly saw Sri Ramakrishna standing in front of her. "Sarada, Sarada," he exclaimed "what are you doing? I am not dead! I have only moved from one room to another."

All the devotees of Ramakrishna now treated Saradamani as their guru. They would consult her when they had any problems or needed advice. When Swami Vivekananda was invited to go to the World Parliament of Religions in America, he first came to Saradamani and, asked for her permission. When Saradamani gave her blessings, only then did Vivekananda decide to leave the shores of India.

Thus did Ma Sarada shoulder the great responsibility of caring for the spiritual welfare of Sri Ramakrishna's disciples. For 24 years after his death, she carried out the aims and objectives of the Ramakrishna Math.

Saradamani's mental penetration was so very keen and her common sense so strong, that even in things supposedly outside her sphere she could give a very sound opinion. During the first Great War, a disciple told the Mother how President Wilson was trying to ensure the peace of the whole world and prevent war in the future. The Mother's quiet remark was, "They all speak through the lips and not from the heart."

In the later part of her life, Ma Sarada suffered from Malaria. In December 1919, she fell seriously ill. On July 26, 1920, she gave up her physical body.

Her teachings were very simple. She would say, "Watch your mind. Until your mind is pure and focused, you will not be able to proceed on the spiritual path. You may have the grace of God, of the Guru, of a Saint on you, but till you have the grace of your own mind, you cannot move forward. Hence do not entangle your mind in useless things. Get engrossed in the Lord's Name."

One of the last teachings she gave to her disciples was this: "If you want peace, don't find fault with others – but rather, find fault with yourself. Learn to make the whole world your own."

My friends, if any person has ten good qualities and one flaw, then our attention rivets towards that flaw. When someone gives a discourse of five thousand words and within that makes an error of two words, our attention is on the errors but, not on the 4998 correctly spoken words. Give up this attitude of fault finding. Every person has one or the other good quality. An individual may be totally seeped in wrong doing, but there will still be some redeeming quality in him. The Mother knew this – and made this her final teaching.

Ma Saradamani was a great saint who combined in herself the roles of a devoted wife, a devoted mother and a wonderful teacher. She did not have children of her own – but thousands of devotees worship her as the Divine Mother, and the Holy Consort of Sri Ramakrishna. She was pure and innocent; her love for her children was infinite. She was, indeed, the embodiment of love, selflessness, sacrifice and purity.

Fragrant be her memory!

Sayings of Ma Saradamani

"I tell you one thing. If you want peace of mind, do not find fault with others. Rather see your own faults. Learn to make the whole world your own. No one is a stranger, my child; the whole world is your own."

* * * * *

"God is one's very own. The more intensely a person practises spiritual disciplines, the more quickly he attains to God."

* * * * *

"The mind is rendered pure as a result of much austerities. God who is purity itself cannot be attained without austerities."

* * * * *

"As wind removes a cloud, so does the Name of God disperse the cloud of worldliness."

* * * * *

"As you smell the fragrance of a flower by handing it or the smell of sandalwood by rubbing it against a stone, so you obtain spiritual awakening by constantly thinking of God."

* * * * *

"One who makes a habit of prayer will easily overcome all difficulties."

* * * * *

"Can you call a person who is devoid of compassion a human being? He is a veritable beast."

* * * * *

"Ordinary human love results in misery. Love for God brings blessedness."

Some Books by Ma Sarada

- *Sri Sarada Devi, The Holy Mother:* Her Teachings And Conversations by Sarada Devi, Swami Adiswarananda and Swami Nikhilananda
- *Teachings of Sri Sarada Devi: The Holy Mother*
- *Ma Sarada Smaranika*
- *Gospel of the Holy Mother: Sri Sarada Devi*

Some Books on Ma Sarada

- *Sri Sarada Devi, the Holy Mother* – Swami Tapasyananda
- *Holy Mother Sri Sarada Devi* – Swami Gambhirananda
- *The Holy Mother as I Saw Her* – Swami Saradeshananda
- *Sri Sarada Devi: the Great Wonder*, a Compilation of Revelations, Reminiscences and Studies – by Monks, Savants, Scholars, Devotees Apostles
- *Holy Mother* – Being The Life Of Sri Sarada Devi, Wife Of Sri Ramakrishna And Helpmate In His Mission – by Swami Nikhilananda
- *A Short Life of Holy Mother* – by Swami Pavitrananda

Guru Gobind Singh

Guru Gobind Singh was a prophet of valour and *shakti*. His life is writ in sacrifice. He sacrificed his all – his sons, his wealth, his life – in the service of India and India's teeming millions. As the Founder of the great Khalsa tradition, he is enshrined in the hearts of millions of Sikhs, who still live by his ideals. He taught that within everyone is a hidden font of *shakti*. This *shakti*, he said, must be unfolded for the service of India and suffering humanity.

Guru Gobind Singh

Gurudev Sadhu Vaswani once said, "If I turn back the pages of history and reflect on the troubles and trials that Hindus have had to face, the eyes of many of you will be filled with tears".

Sadhu Vaswani, of course, spoke with intense feeling born of experience. The Hindu community in this land has almost faced extinction in the past. Even once again, today, the Hindus are not very well-integrated and strong. But, I believe, the day is not far when Hinduism, will shine in all its glory. Today, one brother is desperate to fight with another. Today, one Hindu brother is living a life of rich luxury and on the other hand, another Hindu brother goes hungry. The Hindu community, today, is going through a difficult phase. But soon the day will dawn – the day when the community will evolve and blossom. Through this community God has to perform His great work, because Hinduism has a rich spiritual treasure – the treasure of true *Atma shakti* – spiritual strength. That is why God Himself has protected this community time and again.

Today, I would like to tell you about one of the great Gurus of the Sikhs – the tenth and last Guru. A warrior, a poet, and a spiritual leader, his establishment of the military order of the Khalsa is considered as one of the most important events in the history of Sikhism.

Guru Gobind Singh was born in Patna in 1666 AD. He was the only son of Guru Tegh Bahadur, the ninth guru, and his wife, Mata Gujri. He was named Gobind Rai – and it is said, that his birth and his spiritual power were prophesied by a Muslim *fakir*, who announced that the child would be a saviour of the Faith; the *pir* also travelled to Patna to see the child and bless him.

Gobind Rai spent his childhood in Patna. When he was eight, he was taken to Anandpur, (then known as Chak Nanaki), a city founded by his father, where he learnt Sanskrit and Arabic, as well as Punjabi, Braj and Persian. A Rajput warrior was also employed to train him in military skills and horse riding. During these years, Gobind Rai saw very little of his father, as the Guru was busy in the struggles against the persecution of Hindus by the Mughals.

He was barely 9 years old, when his father was executed by Aurangzeb. The Guru had refused to convert to Islam, and he was beheaded by Aurangzeb, even while he was trying to negotiate religious freedom for Hindus and Sikhs. His head was put on the public square to deter the people from objecting to

Aurangzeb's policies. The beheading of Guru Tegh Bahadur frightened many of his disciples, some of whom even refused to acknowledge themselves as his followers, in order to avoid persecution. A disciple called Bhai Jaita (later Bhai Jivan Singh) brought Guru Tegh Bahadur's head to Anandpur, and narrated the story of his death and the fear among the Guru's followers in Delhi.

Guru Gobind Singh resolved to free the Hindus from the tyranny of the Mughals. He decided that the best way to do this would be to inculcate the martial spirit among his followers. Guru Tegh Bahadur had ordained his son as the next guru, even before his departure to Delhi. Gobind Rai was formally installed as the Guru on the Baisakhi, on November 11, 1675.

He grew up from ordinary bearings to be a great hero. When he was eighteen, Sri Ram Charan of Lahore offered his daughter Sundari in marriage to him. Four years later, their first son Ajit was born. Ajit was followed by 3 more sons.

Guru Gobind Singh brought about great changes in the religious life of his followers. He preached equality of all men. He taught the people that the low and the high, the rich and the poor are all one. In order to translate this into action, the concept of *langar* (fellowship meals) was introduced, where, without distinction of caste, creed, colour, all men sat together at one place and ate their meals on the floor.

Guru Gobind Singh wanted the Sikhs to form a well-knit military community. In 1699, he sent for all his followers to assemble at Anandpur. Thousands of faithful Sikhs congregated to hear him and carry out his commands.

"Who are you?" he asked them.

"We are your faithful disciples," they answered.

"Who am I?" he asked them.

"You are our Beloved Guru and we will carry out your *hukum*," they replied.

All of a sudden Guru Gobind Singh drew out his sword and proclaimed: "For the good of mankind, a human sacrifice has to be offered to Kali. Is there any one among you who is ready to offer himself as a sacrifice?"

There was at first an uncomfortable silence and then one man rose up! The Guru led him into an enclosure. After a while, the Guru emerged out of the enclosure, his sword dripping with blood, and asked for a second sacrifice. Similarly a third, a fourth and a fifth responded to his fiery call.

Then the Guru came out and declared that with these five dear ones who came forward to offer their lives as a sacrifice, the Khalsa Panth was established. The five volunteers emerged unscathed, safe and sound from the enclosure, and were proclaimed as the *panj piyare* – five dear ones. The Guru anointed them with holy water called *amrit* and named them *singh* or lion. This was when he himself came to be called Gobind Singh. He commanded the Khalsa to adopt the 5 K's –

1. Kirpan or sword
2. Kangan or iron bangle
3. Kesa or hair
4. Kanga or comb
5. Kaccha or tight wear

He made them vow, that they would read from the *Guru Granth Sahib* daily and would regard all as their brothers – and be ever ready to extend their hand of helpfulness to people.

The Khalsa movement grew rapidly.

Aurangzeb, the King of the Mughal dynasty, passed away. As a human being, Aurangzeb had many good qualities. He lived a simple life, he ate simple food, lived a pure life, kept away from sex and kept busy all the time. He would make caps with his own hands, read books and would read the Holy Quran Sharif daily. But alas! He was embroiled in religious persecution and forcible conversions. He was a man of strict beliefs. He failed to understand that the Divine light of God shone in all religions, all faiths and all scriptures. He was against the Hindu faith. He was fanatical about converting Hindus into Muslims.

Guru Gobind Singh thought it was his duty to stand up against these tortures inflicted by Aurangzeb. He took to the battlefield to protect the Hindus.

As the darkness of religious persecution had spread all over India, cruelty and injustice was being meted out to the Hindus. On one occasion, while meditating on the mountain top, the Guru heard a voice, "My dear, now it is time for you to come out on to the battlefield." Leaving his meditation, he followed the voice. He came down to the battlefield and started a mighty movement.

Guru Gobind Singh's army although small, had tremendous fortitude and courage. If we look back in history, the Mughal empire of which Aurangzeb was so proud, is no more. But the empire for which the great Guru fought, still throbs with life today. He is still seated on a million thrones. The heart of each and every devotee is his throne.

One day, as Guru Gobind Singh was resting after the evening prayers, two *pathans* stealthily crept into his tent.

One of them stabbed Guru Gobind Singh, fatally wounding him. Soon he received another blow. The wound was immediately sutured but the Guru could not be saved.

He knew now that his end was near and instructed his disciples not to mourn over his death. He proclaimed that there would henceforward be no more human gurus; instead, the *Guru Granth Sahib* would now be the Eternal Guru of the Sikhs after him.

My friends, Gurudev Sadhu Vaswani said that Guru Gobind Singh was a *yogi* on one hand, and a great warrior on the other. He raised an army consisting of 80,000 young men. He built four forts. Guru Gobind Singh was a poet too. His *bani* is still recited with devotion and fervour. He was devoted to God and in this devotion he found immense happiness.

Guru Gobind Singh was a true leader. A true leader, as we know, is one who lives for his fellowmen. A true leader is the father of his fellowmen. Guru Gobind Singh loved the Sikhs dearly. He was a saint. He would serve the poor and was a friend of the sad and the lonely, that is why he was called a King. His life was filled with love and laughter. Around him assembled poets, painters, scholars — Anandpur became a spiritual, physical, emotional centre for the people. Every day in Anandpur was like a New Year's Day. It was a centre of harmony and joy.

He was only 42 years old when the Call came to him, but in this short span he created a revolution in Sikhism. He completed the compilation of the *Guru Granth Sahib;* he was a warrior, a poet, and a spiritual leader. His establishment of the military order Khalsa is considered as one of the most important events in the history of Sikhism. He fought no less than 14 battles with the Mughals and their allies, and won all of them. He lost all his four sons in the course of these wars, but still remained firm in his fight for justice and religious freedom. He was indeed, a great souled leader, an inspiring guru.

Long live his memory!

Sayings of Guru Gobind Singh

"The greatest comforts and lasting peace are obtained, when one eradicates selfishness from within."

* * * * *

"The ignorant person is totally blind; he does not appreciate the value of the jewel."

* * * * *

"God Himself is the Forgiver."

* * * * *

"Without the Name, there is no peace."

* * * * *

"Without the Guru, no one has found the Lord's Name, O my Siblings of Destiny."

* * * * *

"Those who meditate on the Name of the Lord obtain all peace and comforts."

* * * * *

"Let everyone hail and praise the True Guru, who has led us to find the treasure of the Lord's devotional worship."

* * * * *

"Day and night, meditate forever on the Lord."

* * * * *

"There is no friend, other than the Name of the Lord, the Lord's humble servants reflect upon this and see."

* * * * *

"Serving the True Guru, one finds a lasting peace, the pains of birth and death are removed."

* * * * *

"For this purpose was I born, let all virtuous people understand. I was born to advance righteousness, to emancipate the good, and to destroy all evil-doers root and branch."

Some Books by Guru Gobind Singh

- *Dasam Granth*
- *Jaap Sahib* (meditation)
- *Akal Ustat* (praises of God)
- *Bichitra Natak* (an autobiography)
- *Chandi Charitar*, I and II (the character of Goddess Chandi)
- *Chandi di Var*, including Ardas (a ballad to describe Goddess Durga)
- *Gyan Prabodh* (the awakening of knowledge)
- *Chaubis Avtar* (24 incarnations of Vishnu)
- *Brahm Avtar* (incarnation of Brahma)
- *Rudra Avtar* (incarnation of Shiva)
- *Shabad Hazaray* (ten shabads)
- *Swayyae* (33 stanzas)

Some Books on Guru Gobind Singh

- *Life of Sri Guru Gobind Singh Ji* – by Dalip Singh
- *The Saint-Soldier; Guru Gobind Singh* – by Piara Singh Data
- *Illustrated Stories From the Life of Guru Gobind Singh Ji* – by Ajit Singh Aulakh
- *The Zafarnama of Guru Gobind Singh* – by Jasbir Kaur Ahuja
- *Guru Gobind Singh: A biographical study* – by J. S. Grewal
- *Homage to Guru Gobind Singh* – by Khushwant Singh and Suneet Vir Singh
- *The Warrior Princess 2: The Moving Story of Guru Gobind Singh Through the Eyes of Four Saintly Sikh Warrior Women* – by Harjit Singh
- *Guru Gobind Singh: Personality and Vision* – by S. Gajrani

Durgacharan Nag

*D*urgacharan **Nag,** also known as Nag Mahashay, was a disciple of Sri Ramakrishna Paramahansa. A great soul who chose to serve humanity in silence and without expectation of reward or recognition, he was a true *bhakta*, who lived a hidden life in the Hidden One. He beheld God, he beheld his Gurudev in the poor and the sick, whom he served with dedication. His compassion gave him the healing touch, and many were the afflicted whom he healed with his medical care.

Durgacharan Nag

"All around us is darkness, and the darkness deeper grows", wrote a man of letters not long ago. In the midst of this encircling darkness, saints and *satpurkhas* are shining lights. They have appeared in all ages and all climes. Whatever be their colour, creed, caste, country, they belong to one fellowship, one brotherhood. They all teach that God is One and He is the God of mercy and love. He is the ever-forgiving One. And He is not from us afar. Closer is He to us than breathing, nearer than hands and feet. To be able to contact Him we do not have to go to any particular place – to a Temple or Gurudwara, to a Mandir or Masjid, to a Church or a Synagogue or a Buddhist Vihara. All that we need to do is to close our eyes, shut out the world, and call Him with deep love and longing of the heart – and He will be there, with us.

When we study the lives of the saints and servants of humanity – those that have dedicated themselves to the service of Love and Truth – we learn lessons which we all need to learn – lessons which alone will lend a meaning and significance to life.

Not many of you may have heard the name of Durgacharan Nag: he was a devotee of Sri Ramakrishna Paramahansa. He is also known as Nag Mahashay. Mahashay means a great soul and Durgacharan Nag was truly a great and noble soul. He was born on the August 18, 1846, in a small village in far-off East Bengal, which now forms part of Bangladesh. The watch-word of his life was service. He served in a quiet way. He aspired to live a hidden life in the Hidden God. What about us? We do a little service and then after spending a sleepless night, get up in the morning and scan the newspaper to find if our little service has been noticed. This is not service: this is the very death of service. We seem to have confounded service with show and ostentation. We have forgotten that the true strength of a nation lies in silent service. India needs silent servers – men and women who will serve the poor and lowly, the simple village-folk without any thought of popularity, publicity, name and fame.

There was a man who announced that he would be distributing milk powder among slum-dwellers. The poor people – old men, women and children – were asked to come and stand in rows. The milk-powder tins were brought out, and the poor people waited eagerly to receive their share: but the distribution would not begin. Fifteen minutes passed, half an hour passed. The slum-dwellers became restless. "Why aren't we getting the milk powder as promised?" they wanted to know.

The answer they got made no sense to them: the photographer had not arrived!

The "generous donor" was anxious to have his photograph taken in the act of distributing the milk powder. Until the photographer arrived he could not 'turn on' his generosity.

This, my friends, is not true service! I sometimes feel deeply saddened when I think of the shadows we run after – name, fame, greatness, popularity, publicity. As I said, the true strength of a nation is not in these shows – the true strength of a country, the true strength of a community, the true strength of a society is in those who serve silently.

I remember, one day we were in a garden, sitting at the Lotus Feet of my Beloved Master Sadhu Vaswani, when he pointed to some beautiful flowers and said to us, "Look at the flowers! How beautifully they bloom! But they do it silently. Even so must you serve silently. Flowers spread their fragrance in silence – even so must you serve in silence."

Then pointing to the sun, he said, "The sun, even as it shines, sends life-giving warmth and light to the earth. But it shines silently! And remember, there are millions, billions, trillions, countless number of creatures whose very existence depends upon the sun – but the sun shines silently. Even so must you serve silently!"

It was Abraham Lincoln who said, "When I am gone, may it be said about me that here was a man who plucked out a thistle wherever a flower could be planted." What a noble idea this, for all of us to follow! Let us go about silently plucking thistles, and planting flowers in their place. When we serve in silence, our work is truly blessed – and it will abide in the hearts of many!

Sri Durgacharan Nag served silently, without any thought of reward. He served the sick and the poor and asked for nothing in return. In his mind there was a desire for only one thing – to behold the radiant form of his Gurudev. To him every sick and needy person was a picture of his Gurudev. He served with a prayer that his service might be accepted at the feet of the Guru.

His father's name was Dindayal, who was in the employment of a commercial firm in Calcutta and received a very modest salary. Dindayal was very hard working and honest. A story is told of his early life. Once he was asked to deliver some boats filled with salt to a certain address. It took him two to three days to reach the destined place. During his journey, at night, he would place his boats by the bank of the river and sail by day. One day, on waking up he washed his face and, after freshening up, was about to return to his boats, when suddenly, a thought flashed across his mind: let me dig at this spot. He starts digging. At first, he dug a little and found a gold coin. He was wonder-struck. He dug a little more and found another gold coin, then a third and a fourth.

Finally he found a pot filled with gold coins. He was amazed! But do you know what he did? He immediately ran away from the spot. Panting, he reached the place where his boats were moored and ordered the boatmen, "Hurry up! Let us leave from here". They asked him what was the cause for all the hurry. Dindayal, who was a true and honest man, said, "I dug the ground and found a pot of gold, and there arose in my mind a desire to possess the gold coins. Then I said to myself, 'This treasure is not yours. So, what right do you have to take it away? Surely, someone has hidden this treasure here. If you take it, then it is equivalent to robbery. You should not take what does not belong to you.' And therefore, I decided to run away from there at once. The mind is capable of converting falsehood into truth and vice versa. If I had stayed and let loose the reins of my mind even for a short while, I might have got trapped in the abyss of greed. Hence, it was better I ran away".

Dindayal has taught us a lesson which we all will do well to treasure in our hearts. When thoughts of greed wake up in the heart, we should not tarry. We should run away from the spot as fast as our legs can carry us.

Durgacharan Nag was born in such a pious family. His face was handsome, his hair was curly and he had large lotus eyes. Those who saw him as an infant, would immediately take him in their lap and cuddle him. They felt extremely happy to play with him.

Many people would present the child with lovely gifts, but he would take nothing from anyone. Many would offer him delicious things to eat, but he would refuse them all.

As a child, he loved to gaze and gaze at the stars. When evening drew near, he would wait anxiously for nightfall. At night, when the stars were visible, he would gaze at them and be lost in contemplation.

Have you ever gazed at the stars? I once met a person who told me that many years have elapsed since, he had lifted his eyes upwards and even looked at the sky.

On one occasion, Gurudev Sadhu Vaswani said to me, "There are angels and Gods in the stars. The angels beckon and say to us, "Dear one, you think you belong to this earth? But you are not of this earth! You have come here only for a short stay. You have come here for a very special purpose. Do you recall this special purpose?"

Durgacharan would gaze at the stars for hours on end. He would tell his aunt, "These stars are beckoning me, 'Come, come!' How do I go to them? I long to go and live with them."

When the moon would rise, he would clap and dance with joy. Many times he would go and talk to the flowers. When the trees swayed with the breeze, the child would feel a thrill pass through his frame.

Every evening his aunt would tell him stories from the Ramayana, the Mahabharata and the Bhagavad

Purana. If, some day, she did not tell him a story, he would refuse to sleep. So, the aunt had to tell him a story every night.

There was a time when mothers would narrate stories with a moral to their children. When we were children, our mothers would tell us stories. Many times we would say, "Ma, we are feeling sleepy, so we will not have dinner". Immediately she would say, "Come, I will tell you a story and feed you at the same time. After that you can go off to sleep". The desire to hear the story would make us forget our sleep.

The mother is a transmitter of values. When the child is in the impressionable, moulding stage, it is the mother who can sow seeds of culture and character in his plastic mind. She can infuse in him love for his cultural heritage, traditions and value. But today, mothers are busy doing other things and have forgotten their duties by their children.

The result is that children are glued to the TV screen. Not only does this have a harmful effect on their eye-sight, but it also makes them sluggish and lethargic. What is worse, the impact of the violence and other undesirable elements shown on the TV create an indelible negative impression on young minds.

The way our children are being brought up, brings tears to my eyes. Children do not appear to be the product of India's ancient culture. They appear to be a product of some other imitation-cult. For all this, we only have ourselves to blame: we have not paid enough attention to our children.

Let me appeal to all mothers: tell your children about Sri Rama. Tell them about Sita's purity. Tell them stories about Abhimanyu's courage, about Bhishma Pitamaha, who for the love of his father, sacrificed his claim to the throne and even pledged not to marry. When children hear such stories, they will be deeply influenced by them. These stories are like *sanskaras* which, when sowed in their minds, will reap a rich harvest.

I remember, many years ago, Gurudev Sadhu Vaswani had gone to Shikarpur, Sind, which now forms part of Pakistan. There the people met him with deep love and devotion. He addressed a number of meetings and people came in throngs to listen to his soft flute-like voice. On the last day of his stay, he bade them a fond farewell and came to the railway station to catch a train for Hyderabad-Sind. They were told that the train was late by an hour and a half. On hearing this, the people were overjoyed. They said to Sadhu Vaswani, "God has heard our prayers. He too, wishes that you should be with us a little while longer. Before leaving, kindly give us a farewell message."

On the railway platform, the devotees quickly set up a small stage and Sadhu Vaswani stood on it and delivered his message. Among other things, he said, "O citizens of Shikarpur! All I have to say to you is summed up in these words: You are busy gathering, silver and gold. But you have neglected your richest treasure. Your richest treasure is your children. Take good care of them. Give them a proper upbringing. Sow in their plastic hearts seeds of purity and prayer, simplicity and service, courage and compassion, faith and fortitude. As are the seeds that are sown, so will your children be."

Child Durgacharan Nag would listen to the stories told him by his aunt with deep interest and enthusiasm. The stories had a great impact on him. The love for truth blossomed in his life. Even in play or fun he would never speak an untruth. How many of us can say, that we have always spoken the truth? In olden days, India was revered and respected as a leader of the nations. Why? Because the people of India bore witness to the great ideals of truth and purity. Today, what is the condition of India? You know it better than I do. Any amount of material progress will not make India great. It is only until we, who are Indians, stand up for truth and compassion, that India will once again be acclaimed as a leader of the nations.

Durgacharan Nag never spoke an untruth. And if ever he came to know that some of his friends had lied, he would break his friendship with them. His love for truth was so great.

Gradually this child grew up. He went to study in a village school. After he completed his primary education, he wished to study further. But there was no other school in the village. His father had a job in Calcutta. The child found out that there were many schools in Calcutta. When the father came to the village from the city, the child said to him, "Father, please take me to Calcutta, I wish to study further".

Sadly, due to financial constraints the father could not accede to his request. The child would not give up. He made enquiries and was informed of a school ten miles away from the village. But his people at home would not give him permission to travel so far. His aunt said to him, "You will be unable to walk this long distance day after day. It is too much! So, forget about school." Now, Durgacharan Nag was a child of determination. The next morning, he got up and left the house. He walked ten miles to reach the school. He said to the headmaster, "I want to study in this school. Will you accept me?"

In the meantime, in his absence, members of his family searched for him here and there, and could not find him. They were worried beyond words. When he returned home in the evening, his aunt and others were very happy and relieved to see him. His aunt hugged him and said, "We have been wondering since the morning, where you were. Come and eat something. You mustn't have eaten anything all day." When the child told her about his visit to the school, the aunt said, "My child, you have won a seat in the school with your determination."

This little child would walk ten miles to school and ten miles back everyday. He had to face several hardships, but so intense was his thirst for knowledge that he did not mind the physical discomfort. On one occasion during the rainy season, he skid down a slope and fell into a pond. He tried to rescue himself several times, but failed. Finally he began chanting the Name of God. We should also cultivate this habit. Whenever, we find ourselves in a difficult situation which we cannot handle, let us turn our gaze upwards and inwards and chant the Holy Name.

A similar incident occurred in the life of Sadhu Vaswani. He was barely three or four years old when, one sultry afternoon, he stood outside his house. All around, people were enjoying their siesta, in their cool mud-houses. A fierce-looking, giant-sized Pathan appeared and, before he knew it, child Vaswani felt a rough hand catch hold of his neck and stuff him into a pit of darkness. It took the child a long minute to realise that he was inside the Pathan's flowing *salwar* (loose-fitting trousers).

"Help me, God! O save me from this darkness, I pray Thee," pleaded child Vaswani.

The Pathan, who had thought of kidnapping him, found passers-by eyeing suspiciously the movements in his *salwar*, as child Vaswani kept struggling and praying. To avoid the suspicions of the onlooking people he pulled the child out of the darkness and, placing him on a doorstep, vanished as suddenly as he had appeared.

A similar miracle happened with Durgacharan Nag. The Holy Name of God gave him strength. He tried one last time and finally pulled himself out of the pond!

One day, he found an alternative way to get to school. It was a short-cut, but he had to cross a forest. He started going to school through the short-cut. People warned him, "There are many wild animals in the forest. Are you not frightened of them?" To this Durgacharan Nag answerd, "Krishna is with me. Gopal is with me. Govind is with me. Mukund is with me. Hari is with me. Then, why should I be frightened? On entering the forest I call out, 'Gopal, Govind, Mukund, Hari, You are with me, aren't You?' I get the answer, 'Yes, I am with you'. Then, why should I fear?"

For years, through heat and cold, rain and storm, he continued to go to school. In all this period, he missed school only twice.

When he was fifteen years old, he was married to a girl of eleven years. As it was the custom in those days, after marriage, the bride returned to her parents' home as she was too young. Later, she would come to live with her husband when they both grew up. Five months after his marriage, Durgacharan Nag moved to Calcutta, where he joined the Campbell Medical School.

But again, due to financial constraints, he had to discontinue his schooling. He then studied Homeopathy under Dr. Bhaduri, a renowned physician. While he was at Calcutta, his wife met with a sudden, unexpected death. The news of her death greatly saddened Durgacharan Nag.

Deeply grieved at the loss, he started devoting more time to the study of religious books and meditation. Often in the nights he would go to the *samasan ghat* – cremation ground – and sit there for hours together. The funeral pyres would remind him of the transitory nature of human existence.

He would often reflect: life has no meaning. All this is vanity. The things we are running after are mere shadows. We are chasing shadow-shapes of money, name, fame: we lose our precious energy by indulging in sensual pleasures. Finally, man has to go to the crematorium and his body is burnt in the fire and reduced to a handful of ash. God alone is the One Truth of Life. Without God, life is a wilderness. But the question of all questions is: what is the way to God? How do I reach Him? Who will show me the way?

Many *fakirs*, sages and *sanyasis* came to the crematorium to do their 'Sadhana'. He met them and put to them the question: what is life? He noticed that the efforts of these *fakirs* and *sanyasis* were aimed only at acquiring 'Siddhis' or magical and occult powers. That was the only reason for their 'Sadhana' or 'Tapasya'. He was in search of someone who would show him the truth, someone who would show him the path that led to God.

In the meantime, Durgacharan Nag acquired knowledge about Homeopathic medicine. Dr. Bhaduri was surprised to see his quick progress. He noticed that his young pupil was a genius in diagnosis and had an intuition in selecting the right medicine. He did not demand a fee for his services. Whatever people offered him, he accepted in joy and with contentment.

He continued to serve the poor and the sick. He would often take a small bag of medicines in his hand and go about giving free medicines to the needy. Often, he would bring food packets from his house to feed the poor patients. He was a special kind of doctor!

One day, he went to a house where he saw a sick person lying on his bed with no one to take care of him. He said to the man, "I will take care of you." He served him diligently. At night, he visited him again. It was the season of winter. There were many holes in the roof of the house where that poor patient lay in pain. Through those holes, a strong breeze entered the house. Durgacharan Nag saw that the poor man did not even have a blanket with which to cover himself. He took his own shawl and spread it over the sick man and said to him, "Your need is greater than mine. Cover yourself with this shawl and feel warm and cozy. I will come and see you again tomorrow." The poor patient was amazed by this kind gesture. He whispered, "Doctor, please do not give me your shawl. I am used to passing my nights without a shawl or a blanket." But Durgacharan Nag would not hear it, and insisted on leaving his shawl behind. When he reached home that night, his father asked him, "Where is your shawl?" Durgacharan Nag replied, "Father, I saw a poor, sick man who had no blanket with which to cover himself. So, I gave him my shawl." On hearing this, the father lost his temper and said to him, "How will I get money to keep on buying shawls for you? See that you do not repeat this again!"

The father was even more vexed when he observed that his son devoted more and more time to spiritual practice and service of the sick. He thought of getting his son re-married. Durgacharan Nag pleaded with his father not to force him into the bondage of marriage a second time. But the father was firm in his resolve and Durgacharan Nag reluctantly agreed. Soon Durgacharan Nag was married to a girl called Sharatkamini.

A few days later, he visited another patient. He saw him lying on the floor, and said to himself, "There are two beds in my house. I need only one." Immediately, he went home and took one cot to the hut of the poor patient, saying, "You will feel better with this." He completely identified himself with the poor and sick. In return, he would take no payment, no reward from anyone. He believed that what he gave to others was being given to him by God.

In Calcutta, there were many rich people. One of the wealthy families was that of the Pals. They regarded

Durgacharan Nag as their family doctor. One day, a female member of the family, contracted cholera. Durgacharan Nag gave her several medicines, but they had no effect on her. The family called in Dr. Bhaduri for consultation. He was told concerning the medicines prescribed by Dr. Durgacharan and he said, "The medicines that Durgacharan Nag has prescribed are perfect. Please continue with the same medication." Durgacharan Nag continued to treat the woman with determination and, by God's Grace, she recovered fully. Now, the rich family, to express their gratitude towards Dr. Durgacharan Nag, presented him with a silver box filled with money. But, he said, "The medicines I gave cost so little: I cannot accept this gift." He refused to accept the silver box. The family felt that the doctor had found the amount insufficient. So they added more money to the box and once again offered it to him. Durgacharan Nag once again refused to accept it. When the father heard of this, he was livid with rage. He said, "I work from morning till night for a mere pittance. And when you are being given so much money, how can you refuse to accept it? You are absolutely stupid." Durgacharan Nag calmly replied, "Father, I want to remain stupid – for I cannot sell myself for the sake of money." Durgacharan Nag was fortunate in having a wife like Sharatkamini. She understood her husband and his aspirations: she encouraged him to walk on the Path of Truth and Compassion.

Compassion was the one ideal very dear to his heart. He never harmed an insect. When he walked, he was always vigilant lest he stepped on an ant or a worm. Once he bought from a fisherman a large basket of live fish and immediately released them in the waters of the lake. As the fish leapt in the waters, his heart danced like a wave on the surface of an ocean.

He did not wish even to pluck a leaf. Once a cluster of branches damaged the wall of his cottage. Someone offered to cut the branches but he said, "Is it fair to destroy something that you cannot create?"

On another occasion, a cobra appeared in his courtyard. Fearing it would bite and harm someone, the neighbours wanted to kill it. Immediately Durgacharan Nag said, "It is not this cobra, but the cobra of the mind that harms and damages our life." Then folding his hands, he spoke lovingly to the cobra. "O dear one, your abode, your home is in the forest. Go back and live there and leave this humble abode for us!" Amazingly, the cobra retraced its steps and left for the forest. Seeing the cobra returning to the forest, Durgacharan Nag said, "If you do not harm anyone, no one will harm you."

Within him was a deep desire to attain to God-realisation. This desire to realise God did not allow him to rest. He longed to be shown the Way. He came into contact with Sri Ramakrishna Paramahansa at last. The disciple found his Guru and the journey to God began. And he beheld the vision of the Lord in the poor and the sick. He served them sincerely with all he had, with his medical expertise, his compassion, his little wealth, his physical and emotional support. In the evening, when he returned home, his pockets would be empty. Many nights he would have nothing to eat. To fill his stomach, he would just eat some puffed rice. But he was happy, for he had the realisation that we have not come to this earth to earn wealth, but to attain to the Lord, to know our true Self, to serve the poor and the sick and thus earn their blessings.

Durgacharan Nag passed away on December 27, 1899. Two days before his death, he said, "Sri Ramakrishna has come to take me!"

Yes, Sri Ramakrishna came to receive his dear, devoted disciple, Durgacharan Nag. He passed away gazing at the Master's beautiful picture and chanting His Holy Name!

Homage to this simple pilgrim of the Little Way!

Dharam Devi

Dharam Devi was a child prodigy, who, from the tender age of three, was smitten with utter love and devotion for Sri Krishna. Her devotion enabled her to reach those higher states of consciousness, which took her close to the presence of the Divine. It also made her aware of profound truths which are out of reach for barren intellects. She was indeed, the very embodiment of love and devotion for her Shyam Sunder.

Dharam Devi

What is the greatest wealth of life? To some people, lakhs and crores of Rupees is the greatest wealth. But life's greatest treasure is not gold, silver, materials, goods or lakhs and crores of Rupees. If that were true, then human beings should be able to carry these lakhs and crores of Rupees with themselves to the life beyond!

Life's greatest wealth is not prestige and power, high positions, name and fame. Life's greatest wealth is devotion. Devotion is the true wealth of an individual.

May I speak to you of such a devotee? She was a devotee of Shyam, Lord Krishna. Her heart always yearned for the Lord. She cried again and again, "Shyam! How can I live without a glimpse of You?"

We too, sometimes, utter these words, but our words are hollow. Within our hearts, the pain of separation from the Lord has not yet arisen. When we realise that we have been separated from our Beloved, then from within the very depths of our being this cry will emerge. Pain arises only in wounded hearts. Worldly luxuries, comforts and sensory pleasures will cease to satisfy us.

One such devotee of the Lord was Dharam Devi. Even as a child, from the tender age of three, when she looked at the picture of Shyam Sunder, Lord Krishna, she was enchanted by the Lord. Her parents would ask, "What has happened to you? You have been staring at this picture for long and your eyes are filled with tears. What is the reason?" Dharam Devi would reply, "Mother! Father! Lord Krishna has sent me to this world and has asked me to spread the joy of pure love and devotion. This world is surrounded by the darkness of ignorance and people are unhappy. They are drowned in sadness. They need this great message." Her shining face and the spontaneous flow of words shocked the parents. For the child asserted again and again, "I have been sent to dispel ignorance and spread the gospel of love."

As a child, she never played and jumped about like other children. Instead, she would gather all her friends and tell them, "Come! Come! We all will play *Raas Leela* (Lord Krishna's games)." Many times she would pretend to be Krishna, or she would ask her friends to pose as Krishna while she would pose as Radha. Thus, she arranged the *raas garbaa* – the dance of Lord Krishna – and the neighbours were utterly amazed by it. When she played the part of Lord Krishna in the dance, everyone felt as though the Lord Himself were visible. When she played the part of Radha, they felt as though Radha had come down to the earth, in her form.

When she was about five years old, one day she lost her consciousness and fell into a trance. Her consciousness flowed upwards. For ten hours she stayed in this condition. After ten hours, when she opened her eyes, she said, "Where have I come? I was in the world of Sri Krishna. I was among the simple cowherds. I was sitting at the Lotus Feet of the Lord. Now where have I come?"

Dharam Devi was a petite and short girl, but she was very energetic. She had mischievous eyes and a radiant face. She spoke with the light of wisdom and experience. If any questions were posed before her, she never paused or delayed even for a moment, in replying. She would give a prompt reply to difficult questions posed to her. Even when she was just seven years old, people would be amazed at her intelligent responses.

One day, Swami Ramdas, a saint of Anand Ashram, whom his disciples called Papa Ramdas, came to meet Dharam Devi. He had heard a lot about her.

He saw the Divine Light shining in her. Such wonderful words poured out from her lips! He asked Dharam Devi, "Child! Tell me, what is the teaching given to us in the Bhagavad Gita?" Immediately the girl replied, "The Bhagavad Gita teaches us Divine knowledge."

Papa Ramdas then asked her what made her speak these words. To which she replied, "Not me, but God speaks through me. Like you, even I am listening." Papa Ramdas asked, "What should a man do to obtain God?" Dharam Devi replied, "If one desires to find God, then he must be in the company of saints and sing the praise of God." Papa Ramdas asked, "What is the mark of a true saint?" Dharam Devi replied, "A true saint is one from whom the Divine Light radiates and every word spoken by him leaves a deep impact on our hearts."

Swami Ramdas continued, "To see Sri Krishna what does one have to practise?" She replied, "Love and devotion. If you wish to behold the beauteous face of Sri Krishna, then cultivate deep love for Him." Now the saint countered, "In that case, are the mind and intelligence of no use?" This was a difficult question, but the child replied, without hesitating even a moment, "Mind and intelligence are not useless. Through intelligence one can come to know what is true and what is false, what is permanent and what is temporary. Once we realise that truth and permanence is Sri Krishna, then all else is false. Wealth, reputation, high positions, servants, money, everything is false. Truth is the One Krishna. Then you should lay your intelligence at the Lotus Feet of Sri Krishna. The more one tries to understand Sri Krishna, the more complicated it gets. Therefore, do not try to understand Him by means of your intelligence. Instead, one should wrap up one's mind and intelligence and place them at the Lotus Feet of Lord Sri Krishna."

What a wonderful thought the child has given us! We must love Sri Krishna more and more. Say to the Lord, "O Lord, I love You and wish to love You more and more. So much so, that one day I may merge in this love, I may be concealed by this love and become invisible."

To obtain Sri Krishna, one does not have to understand Him. One can find Him only with love and devotion. Love Sri Krishna from more to more. Speak to Him. Tell Him, 'My Beloved, You are so sweet, You are so beautiful. That is why people call You Shyam Sunder. There is magic in Your flute. Play the flute for me too.' In this way, keep talking to Lord Sri Krishna with pure love and devotion.

Love Sri Krishna; say to Him, 'Krishna, my Shyam, my Beloved, in the lanes of Vrindavan You played *Raas Leela,* Your games. Come to my temple and dance, come and sing to me. Enchant me with Your songs. Make my heart, which is barren, into a garden where new flowers of Your love bloom. With those fresh blossoms, my Lord, may I pray to You.'

Wrap up your mind and intelligence and place them at the Lotus Feet of the Lord and tie yourself to the Lord with the thread of love.

Papa Ramdas asked Dharam Devi, "Child, tell me which is the best vision of Sri Krishna? The vision of Sri Krishna in His supernatural form, playing the flute or the vision of Sri Krishna in the world, in every human being: which is the best vision?"

Dharam Devi replied, "See Him in all, everywhere. In every atom is my Beloved. This is the true vision."

On another occasion someone asked Dharam Devi, "If Sri Krishna is in every atom, it also means that He is in the stone too. Then how shall I put my foot on the stone?" Dharam Devi immediately replied, "If Sri Krishna is in the stone, then He is also present in the foot. You have placed Krishna on top of Krishna, then what is the difficulty?"

Child Dharam Devi sang songs which caused such intoxication that people around her would start dancing. Beautiful songs poured out of her lips as though someone else was singing through her. One day, with closed eyes she prayed to the Lord, "My Beloved, keeping awake at nights I have called out for You! You have still not come to me. I am ready to shower everything I have on You. I do not desire salvation. I only desire to find Your Lotus Feet." She said, "My Lord, You are dark, that is why You can hide."

Once a man came to the little child and said, "Teach me to meditate." She took him to an empty room, closed the door and said, "Come, I shall teach you to meditate." After a short while, people heard songs being sung in praise of the Lord:

'Govinda Madhava Gopala Keshava
Hey Nanda Mukunda, Nanda Govinda Radhe Gopala.'

When she was about 7 years old, she saw an old man, Nanak Chand, who could not walk erect. His back was bent.

"Why don't you walk erect?" she said to him.

She then touched his back. Immediately the man stood erect.

Tears flowed down his cheeks and he fell at her feet.

Dharam Devi never allowed anyone to touch her feet. If anyone did so, in return she would immediately touch his or her feet.

My friends, singing the Name of the Lord, accompanied by music, has a potent power. It calms and steadies our fleeting mind, uplifts our consciousness. Come, let us bow down to the feet of this devotee, Dharam Devi, and request the Lord to grant us also, that pure love and utter devotion. I wish we too, could walk on the path of devotion and see the face of Sri Krishna in each and everyone, serve the poor, the downtrodden, animals and birds, receive their blessings and make our human birth worthwhile.

Bhakta Ramdas

Bhakta Ramdas of Daakur was indeed a blessed soul, greatly beloved of Dwarkanath – Sri Krishna himself. This humble devotee of the Lord made it his life's mission to walk to Dwaraka on foot every *Ekadashi* day, for a *darshan* of his beloved Sri Krishna. When he could no longer undertake the journey due to old age, Sri Krishna went with him to the village of Daakur, much to the consternation of the pundits of the temple. Through this simple devotee's life, the Lord taught the world, that we only have to surrender ourselves to His Will – and He will take care of everything that we need.

Bhakta Ramdas

There is a village near Dwarka called Daakur. Even today, there are many pilgrims, who stop at Daakur and pay their respects to Bhakta Ramdas and then proceed to Dwarka. Bhakta Ramdas was born in Daakur. Even as a child, he would meditate on the form of Lord Krishna. The Name of the Lord was on his lips all the time. When he was eating, drinking, sleeping, or studying — all the time he would utter the sacred *mantra* — 'Hare Krishna, Hare Krishna, Krishna, Krishna, Hare Hare. Hare Shyama, Hare Shyama, Shyama Shyama, Hare Hare!'

People knew that Bhakta Ramdas did not have a job or occupation of any kind. He had no means of earning a living. They would call him and say to him, "If you need food, we will give you some!" Ramdas would say, "Instead of food, give me some grains." They would give him grains and he would take what he had received home to his wife, saying, "I have brought grains. Now prepare some food and feed as many as you can with it."

He was filled with deep devotion for Lord Krishna. Every *Ekadashi*, he would aspire to reach Dwarka. It would take him some days to complete this journey. He would walk steadily and at every step he repeated the Name of Lord Krishna. He would take with him a small Tulsi plant, and move on his pilgrim path.

If perchance, someone saw him along their path, they would halt and give Ramdas a lift in their bullock cart. Sometimes, he would come across a horse rider who would give him a ride. So, whatever the manner of travel, he would see to it that he reached Dwarka on the sacred *Ekadashi* day. Espying Dwarka from afar, his heart would jump with joy. Tears of delight would pour forth from his eyes. Upon entering Dwarka, the first thing he would do was to go and bathe in the Gomti River. After bathing he would, from afar, with folded hands, greet Sri Krishna.

Ramdas would then approach the temple, lay his body supine at the threshold, bow down to pay his homage, and then enter the Lord's abode. He would then make a beeline for Sri Krishna's *murthi* (idol), sit at the feet of the statue and pray, "O Lord, please break asunder this chain of birth and death, so that there is no distance between You and me. Make me one with You. Let this be my final birth. Release me from the cycle of birth and death. My Lord, please ensure that in future, I may always be at Your Lotus Feet, gazing at Your Beauteous Face."

Then, Bhakta Ramdas would return to his village. This went on for twenty-five years. For twenty-five years, Ramdas walked by foot to behold his Dwarkanath. He never missed even a single *Ekadashi*. Now old age was catching up on him. He did not have enough strength in his body to accomplish this journey. It was painful for him to go on foot. So, he thought he would go for the last time to the temple and bid goodbye to Lord Krishna.

When he came to the temple, he looked at the statue of his Lord Shyam Sundar – The Beautiful One – and called out to Him with tears in his eyes, "O my God, now my body does not have the strength of yore. I feel as though this is my last visit. The thread of my life is in Your safe Hands. I may have to bid farewell to You. But I lay a request at Your Feet. You may keep me wherever You wish, but please do not ever keep me far from Your love. I survive on Your love. If I don't receive Your love even for a moment, I will wither and die."

While calling out to the Lord, tears rolled down his cheeks. He was sure he would not be able to come to Dwarka again. Even as he wept and uttered his fervent prayer, his eyes were heavy with tears, and he fell into a weary sleep. In his dream he saw Sri Krishna. Sri Krishna came to him and said, "Wake up Bhakta Ramdas! Why are you upset? What is it that worries you?"

"Lord, I have only one worry," said Ramdas. "For so many years, I have come to see You on every *Ekadashi*. But now, I shall not be able to come any more. I cannot live without You."

Sri Krishna looked at him with mercy and said, "My dear one, do not be upset. For the past twenty-five years, on every *Ekadashi* you came to Me. You have not missed a single turn. You have shed tears of love and longing! I cannot think of a more valuable gift than this. If you cannot come to Me, why don't you take Me along with you?"

Bhakta Ramdas was astonished to hear this, "Take You with me? My Beloved, my Lord, how can I take You along with me? You are established in this temple, how can I take You with me?"

Sri Krishna said, "My dear one, it is not as difficult as you think. In the corner of the temple is a shed, in which there is a carriage. Near the shed, there is a stable where you will find horses. At night, when the priests are asleep, you can tether the horses to the carriage, place Me in it and take Me away. I want to go along with you. I do not wish to stay away from you."

Is it not wonderful, that, Sri Krishna is prepared to do everything for the sake of His devotees! There must have been thousands of devotees visiting Dwarka every day, every week. But the sincere devotion of this one, humble, unassuming devotee drew Sri Krishna towards him. So it was that Sri Krishna said to him, "If you cannot come to Me, how will I be able to stay without you? I cannot be away from you. You come to Me on every *Ekadashi* day and go back to your village the very next day. I anxiously wait for the next *Ekadashi* to come, when I can have a glimpse of My true devotee."

Yes, the Lord too, yearns for His devotees. We, in our ignorance, think that it is only the devotee who longs for the Lord. But the Lord Himself yearns for a sincere devotee.

Bhakta Ramdas opened his eyes. He remembered the dream vividly. When darkness fell and the priests retired for the night, Ramdas did as the Lord had directed him to do. He followed all the instructions given by the Lord. He brought the carriage out from the shed and harnessed the horses to it, then he placed the Lord's *murthi* in the carriage; he kidnapped Him!

At dawn, he reached his village. He wondered where he could conceal the Lord. He said to himself, "I do not have enough space in my house. I just have a broken hut. Where can I seat the Lord? Where should I hide Him? If I seat Him in my hut, then in the morning the priests will come and find Him here. Then they will beat me and take Him back!"

He was frightened. So what does he do? Near his village there was a large lake. He puts the statue of the Lord in the lake.

Early next morning the priests entered the temple, and were aghast to find Sri Krishna's statue missing. They wondered who could have removed the statue of the Lord. "Ramdas was the last one here," recollected a priest. "This must be his work. Ramdas had also mentioned that this was his last visit to Dwaraka. Surely, he has escaped with the statue."

The priests further discovered that the carriage was also missing as were the horses from the stable. The trail clearly indicated that the carriage had headed towards the village of Daakur. "It is certainly the work of Ramdas!" they exclaimed, "Ramdas has absconded with the Lord's statue, no one else could have done this."

The priests came to Daakur and caught hold of Ramdas. One priest pulled him by an ear and the next by the other, the third held tight his one hand and the fourth the other. They questioned him, "Tell us, where have you hidden the statue of the Lord."

"If you wish you can check my house," Ramdas cried, "and if you like you could check all the houses in Daakur."

They went to Bhakta Ramdas' hut and failed to find the statue there. They searched every house in Daakur village, but were unable to find the statue. They even checked all the lakes and ponds in the village, but to no avail. Finally, one priest went to a lake, a little away from the village. There he found the statue of the Lord. "The Lord has been found!" he announced.

All the priests were filled with joy, but Ramdas bowed his head in sorrow. "I put in my best efforts to keep You concealed," he cried to the Lord, "but You did not hide Yourself from them. Only You can understand Your *Leela!* Lord, it was You who told me to bring You here, and now, You reveal Yourself to the priests! Your *Leela* is unfathomable."

Then he hears a heavenly voice. It says to him, "Ramdas, do not lose courage. Go and tell the priests that you will pay them gold equivalent to the weight of My statue. Then they will not take Me away from here. If they wish, they can go to Dwarka and make another statue of Krishna, from the gold you give them. You make this deal with them and they will readily and happily accept it!"

"Lord, it is easy for You to say that I should pay them gold equal to Your weight," Ramdas exclaimed. "But I do not have *any* gold with me! Do You know how much gold there is with me? My wife has a tiny ring on her nose made of gold, which is so worn out that I feel it can fall off any day. This nose-ring was given to her by her uncle during our wedding. It is very thin, worn out and hardly worth anything."

The Lord assured Ramdas, "Do not worry my son. Just do what I ask you to. You place the nose-ring on the weighing scale and leave the rest to Me. Then you just sit back and watch what happens!"

Bhakta Ramdas now approached the priests with a request, "I was the one who brought the statue here because the Lord had ordered me to do so. Now He has asked me to give you as much gold as the weight of this statue. Will you then be kind enough to leave the Lord here and go back? You can take the gold to Dwarka and make a new statue of the Lord."

On hearing this, the priests burst out laughing. "From where will you bring the gold?" they enquired. "This whole village cannot have so much gold! Even if *all* the women in the village offered *all* their gold jewellery to be placed on one side of the weighing scale, and we placed the statue of Lord Krishna on the other, the scale will tip in favour of the statue, with your gold being much lighter. How can you imagine that the Lord's statue will be left behind? You say that the Lord Himself asked you to do this. Fine! Bring in gold equal to the weight of the Lord's statue, then we will leave the statue behind."

They were convinced that Ramdas could not substantiate his words. They decided that they would agree to what Ramdas said, if he proved himself.

The news spread like wildfire all over the village. The priests asked for a large-sized weighing scale. The scale had the statue of the Lord placed on one side. The villagers, who used to make fun of Ramdas, now saw one more opportunity to ridicule him. "He is a person who has no food to eat, no clothes to wear," they laughed. "From where is he going to procure so much gold?" they mocked.

The entire village had gathered there. The priests ordered Ramdas, "Go and bring the gold." Ramdas went to his hut and carefully brought his wife's nose-ring. The nose-ring had become so fine that it could have easily slipped through his fingers and fallen, and one would not even have been aware of it. He brought the nose-ring in his closed fist.

He shut his eyes, offered a prayer to Sri Krishna, *"Deen-Bandhu Deena Nath, Meri Dori Tere Hath!* Lord, I did as You asked me to. Now, I am totally in Your Hands." After his prayer, Ramdas placed the nose-ring on the other side of the weighing scale.

Slowly the statue of the Lord began to reduce in size. The people watched in amazement as the statue kept on diminishing in size. The Lord now assumed a miniature form. The scale started going up higher and higher and the tray in which the nose-ring was placed, came lower and lower, until both were on par with each other.

People started clapping with joy and showered flowers on Ramdas, "Jai Bhakta Ramdas, *Jai ho! Jai ho!*" they exclaimed, "Victory to Bhakta Ramdas! Victory to Bhakta Ramdas!" Bhakta Ramdas lifted the statue of Krishna and hid it in his bag. The Lord's statue now started increasing in size and assumed its original form. People watched this miracle.

My dear friends, the Lord performs strange miracles to fulfill the wishes of His devotees. All we need to do is to become puppets in His Hand. All we need to do is to hand over the thread of our life in His hands, and say to him, *"Deen-Bandhu Deena Nath, Meri Dori Tere Hath!"* and He will take care of us! He will never forsake us! That is His Promise!

Sant Purandardas

Purandardas was one of the great singer-saints of South India. Trained to be a jeweller and a businessman, he was enchained by material wealth – in fact, a miser scorned by the people. But the Lord's grace touched him, transforming his life completely. He turned his back on all his accumulated wealth and chose to devote himself to the one true wealth that is eternal, which cannot be stolen, looted or spent away – the treasure of the Name Divine. His songs are the wealth of all true lovers of the Lord, even today.

Sant Purandardas

The sacred land of Karnataka has been home to many saints. One of them was Sant Purandardas. Though he appeared centuries ago, his songs continue to be sung with faith and fervour in South India, till this day.

In his early days, however, there were no indications in his life or personality, of the spiritual stature to which he would rise eventually. To begin with, to all outward appearances, he was just an ordinary man, a householder, a dealer in gems and jewels – and a miser of the first order! Truly, God's ways are mysterious! Sometimes, the grace of God descends on ordinary mortals and, in a flash, they are transformed into heroes and holy men.

Sant Purandardas was born in a rich Brahmin family in 1484. His name was Srinivasa Nayak. His father, Vardappa Nayak, was a well known jeweller. Kings, ministers, wealthy merchants and noblemen would come and buy jewellery from his shop. He was not merely an expert jeweller, but a thoroughly reliable and honest businessman.

When Vardappa Nayak passed away, he left all his wealth, his shop, and his impeccable reputation to his son, Srinivasa Nayak. Srinivasa put forth his best efforts and the business grew from strength to strength.

It was said, that in Karnataka, there was no one to equal Srinivasa in perfect and accurate grading and evaluation of diamonds. So much so, people gave him the title, *Navakoti Narayana*, in praise of his skill and his wealth!

Srinivasa Nayak was completely absorbed in his business. He worked from early morning till late into the evening. His one desire was to make more and more money. He constantly worked on new ideas and schemes to expand his business.

Srinivasa was so obsessed with the desire of accumulating wealth, that he did not wish to spend any money on himself! He was a great miser! He would not give his wife, Saraswati, enough money for household expenses. Saraswati was a devotee of the Lord. She would sit at her *puja* and pray to God, "O Lord, you have blessed my husband with abundant wealth. Bless him with a kind and generous heart."

Their town had this beautiful tradition – that on festive occasions, after taking a dip in the river Seema, everyone was supposed to give away something or the other in charity. The thought of giving anything in charity, horrified Srinivasa. To keep up with the custom, Srinivasa would go to an isolated corner of the river bank to take his ritual bath and return home hastily, before anyone could approach him for alms.

However, on one occasion, he was spotted by a poor Brahmin. The Brahmin pleaded with him for some alms on this auspicious day. Srinivasa found himself in a quandary. On the one hand he did not want to part with his money; on the other, he could not send the Brahmin away empty-handed. He took out a copper coin from his pocket, dropped it on the soil and covered it with his foot. He pretended to have lost his money and started crying like a child. On hearing his cries, many people gathered around him. They saw through his trick, and made fun of him.

His wife was miserable, when she heard about this; she felt sorry for him and continued to pray to the Lord. No prayer ever goes in vain. If you offer a prayer with a heart sincere and lowly, sooner or later, the prayer is sure to be answered.

One day, an old man approached Srinivasa Nayak, saying: "I am a poor Brahmin. I need to perform my son's thread ceremony. Could you kindly donate the money I need for the ceremony?" On hearing the words 'money' and 'donation' Srinivasa began to boil with rage. He retorted, "Who do you think you are? And who do you think I am? Do you think I own a gold mine? Go away from here!"

The Brahmin, however, refused to return empty-handed. He proceeded to relate the tragic story of his life. For a moment, even Srinivasa's heart was touched. He asked the Brahmin to come and see him the following day.

The next day, when the poor Brahmin came, Srinivasa Nayak put him off again, and asked him to return the following day. This went on for six months. The Brahmin would not give up. Finally, Srinivasa gave in. From his safe, he pulled out a few worn-out copper coins and placed them in front of the Brahmin. "Pick out one among these," he said to the Brahmin. Disappointed, the Brahmin refused to take any of the coins. He went to Srinivasa's wife and complained to her.

Saraswati was in despair. She explained to the Brahmin that she was not in a position to help him in any way, for she herself possessed nothing. On hearing this, the Brahmin pointed to Saraswati's nose-ring and said, "Surely, this nose-ring belongs to you. You received it from your parents. Could you not be so kind as to gift it to me?" Saraswati was astonished to hear this. She wondered how the Brahmin knew that the diamond nose-ring was gifted to her by her parents.

Right away, she removed her diamond nose-ring and gave it to the Brahmin. The Brahmin immediately took it to Srinivasa Nayak's shop and said to him, "Will you please tell me the value of this nose-ring? I wish to pledge it!"

Srinivasa was astonished to see the nose ring. He knew that it belonged to his wife: how did it get into the hands of the Brahmin? Controlling his temper, he estimated its value and passed on the amount to the

Brahmin. The Brahmin requested Srinivasa to keep the money with him on interest. Quietly, Srinivasa placed both the nose-ring and money in his safe. His heart seethed with anger. He said to himself, "How could my wife give away such a valuable nose-ring in charity?"

That evening, Saraswati was glad to see her husband back home early. However, her happiness vanished the moment her husband looked her in the face and asked sharply, "What have you done with your nose-ring? Have you given it away?"

Saraswati was petrified with terror. She could not give an answer. "Tell me at once where your nose-ring has gone, or else I will kill you this very moment," thundered Srinivasa.

Fearfully, Saraswati replied, "The grooves of the nose-ring had become worn out with use. Therefore, I have put it away in the safe until I get it repaired."

Srinivasa realised that his wife was lying to him. "Go and bring the nose-ring this very instant," he commanded. "If you are unable to bring it, I will not let you stay in my house even for a single moment."

Trembling with fear, Saraswati went to the kitchen and bolted the door from within. "God," she prayed. "I have not committed a crime. I gave my nose-ring to the old Brahmin in charity and compassion. What shall I tell my husband now? Maybe it is better that I end my life!"

Quickly, she prepared a drink of poison and was about to consume it, when she heard the sound of something dropping on the floor. She bent low to pick it up. She was wonder-struck to find that it was the diamond nose-ring!

She could not understand what was happening. "I had given my nose-ring to the Brahmin," she said to herself. "How did it get back here?"

She threw away the cup of poison and brought the nose-ring and gave it to her husband. He looked at it in disbelief. "How did this nose-ring get here?" he wondered. "I had locked it up in my own safe!" He took the nose-ring, ran to the shop and unlocked the safe. He found the nose-ring missing!

At that moment, his life was transformed. "This can only be the work of the Lord," he exclaimed. "No human being could have performed this feat."

Srinivasa fell on his knees, with tears flowing profusely, and begged God for forgiveness. Barely ten minutes earlier, this individual had been ensnared by the chains of greed; he had been enmeshed in the attachment for wealth. Now, the same Srinivasa decided that he would share all he had with the poor and needy.

The doors of his house were opened to one and all.

The poor came to Srinivasa and he gave food to some, clothes to others; he even gave away his gems and jewels. He kept nothing for himself. "I came to this world empty-handed," he said to himself, "and will return from here leaving even my hands behind. Let me share all that I have with others and spend the remaining days of my life in communion with the Lord."

From then on, Srinivasa led the life of an ascetic, wandering from place to place, living on alms begged from householders. At Pandharpur, he received initiation from a Guru and acquired knowledge at his feet. The Guru bestowed the name Purandara Dasa on him. His *kantha chakra* opened miraculously, and song after song flowed out of his lips. He sang such sweet songs, steeped in devotion, that even today, they are sung with great faith and reverence, in temples and homes of Karnataka, where he is revered as *Karnatak Sangeeta Pitamaha* or the Father of Carnatic Music.

From the wealthy jeweller Srinivasa, trapped in the snare of material wealth, emerged the singing saint Purandardas, whose sole treasure was *Hari Naam*. *Navakoti Narayana* was transformed by the Lord's grace into a great *Narayana bhakta!*

May I share with you a beautiful thought from one of his immortal *bhajans*: "O mind, why do you worry? Why not just meditate on Hari!"

Srinivasa Nayak realised that there is only one true jewel, the jewel of the Name of Hari. He strove to receive this jewel, for he knew that during the final moments of life, it is only this treasure of the Name Divine that would be of any use to him, to carry him forward beyond earthly life.

Let us too, every day, spend some time chanting the Name of God. The Name of God is a great purifier. It will purify us and we too, shall behold the Beauteous Face of the Lord in the lotus of our hearts.

Sayings of Purandardas

"When one is in trouble or in a happy state,
In mental peace or mental aberration,
Good persons crave for the name: Krishna,
Or the eight-lettered *Mantra: Om Namo Narayana.*"

* * * * *

"O! Hari! Destroyer of sorrow! Always let your thousand names be in my heart!
If the name of Purandara's Master is remembered at the final hour of life, there will be true elevation."

* * * * *

"Sing and worship the Lord
Who lies on the serpent and is revered by Narada!

* * * * *

"Don't wander losing your head thinking that your wife and sons will do you good!
When the way is lost and the time to depart comes, Can the wife and sons come (with you)?"

Swami Ugradas

Swami Ugradas is not known to many of us. But he was one of the great souls who was destined to teach great truths to humanity. His name is linked with his devoted disciple, Naabhaji, who was a singer of the spirit. Together, Swami Ugradas and Naabhaji, touched the life of the great saint, Tulsidas, in an unforgettable manner. Our lives are richer and more meaningful, because of this unforgettable encounter!

Swami Ugradas

God works in mysterious ways, to perform his wondrous miracles. From time to time, He sends saints to this earth, to lift the people out of the quagmire of ignorance, evil and delusion. They try to sow and nourish in us, seeds of godliness; they lead us onward, godward.

As I write this, my thoughts move out to a saint, who lived four hundred years ago. He was called Ugradas. He used to hold daily *satsangs*. During one of his *satsangs*, he said something which all of us would do well to reflect on. He said, "People in India are unaware of their precious heritage. Alas! They are ignorant about the life and teachings of many saints, great souls and devotees of the Lord. It is our duty to educate them about such great souls, or else, over a period of time, the lives and teachings of such saints, holy men and devotees will be lost and forgotten! We must not allow this to happen!"

Ugradas had a disciple who was very devoted to him. His name was Naabhaji. Naabhaji had the gift of writing poetry. He also had a melodious voice. When he sang, he inspired, he captivated the hearts of his listeners.

Though Naabhaji was from a lower caste, he had a great devotion for Lord Krishna. His devotion for the Lord was beyond words. He would compose poems in praise of the Lord, and shed unbidden tears of love and longing for the Lord.

Gurudev Sadhu Vaswani used to say to us that one of the characteristics of a true devotee is that when he hears or recites the Name of the Lord, his eyes are filled with unbidden tears. Naabhaji was such a one! He took nine long years to compose a work of devotion which he offered at the feet of Lord Krishna.

Ugradas was very pleased with his dear disciple Naabhaji. He requested him to read a passage from the book. Naabhaji obeyed his Guru's command. As Naabhaji read passage after passage, the heart of Ugradas was touched beyond measure. "This book should be read out to the people!" he exclaimed. Naabhaji asked his Guru to kindly suggest an appropriate title for the book. Swami Ugradas gave the title, *Bhakta Mala*, to this beautiful work.

In those days, Banaras was the heart of spiritual life in this country. Saints and devotees loved to congregate in the holy city. They would hold their *satsangs* in Banaras, where thousands of devotees gathered. Swami Ugradas decided to go to Banaras and share with the people the great treasure written by his dear disciple, Naabhaji.

At Banaras, Swami Ugradas started to hold *satsangs*. The *satsang* drew many devotees, as was usual in the holy city. At that time two other great saints also resided in Banaras. One was Sant Tulsidas, the author of the great epic, *Rama Charita Manas*. And the other, Sant Kabir, whom we know and revere as a weaver-saint. Both these great saints came to know about the work of Naabhaji, and after reading it, praised the book and its author very highly.

Swami Ugradas decided to hold a huge *Bhandara* (fellowship gathering) and sent invitations to all the saints and devotees. Sant Tulsidas received the invitation to attend the *Bhandara*. He said to himself, "I belong to a high caste. How can I attend a *Bhandara* being held by one from a lower caste? This is impossible!"

Swami Ugradas came to know of this.

Arrangements for the *Bhandara* were being made meticulously. Swami Ugradas organised the *Bhandara* in a huge hall where adequate seating arrangements could be made for each and every person invited. Each invitee's name was written and displayed at the place reserved for him. As Sant Tulsidas' name was held in very high esteem, his seat was reserved right at the centre of the hall, at a place of honour.

When news reached Naabhaji that Sant Tulsidas had refused to come to the *langar*, he smiled. He did not feel offended. "It is true, I belong to a lower caste," he admitted. "Why would a saint from a higher caste come to the *langar* of a devotee who belongs to a lower caste?" He therefore, assigned the seat reserved for Sant Tulsidas to another holy man.

Finally the day of the *Bhandara* dawned. Many saints and devotees arrived from various places. All were greeted with great love and respect and were directed to their allocated seats.

Sant Tulsidas heard of the success of the *Bhandara*. He said to himself, "What am I doing here all alone? I have myself written in my *Rama Charita Manas*, the episode where Lord Rama shunned the invitations of *Rishis* and princes and accepted the invitation of Shabri, an outcast woman. Sri Rama not only visited her humble abode but he also partook of the berries, initially tasted by Shabri! I have written all this about Lord Rama, and yet I claim to belong to a higher caste, and am refusing to attend the *Bhandara* organised by Naabhaji, who belongs to a lower caste. How can I do such a thing?"

Determined to make up for his disrespectful attitude, Sant Tulsidas immediately left for the *Bhandara*.

On arriving there, he saw that the hall was packed to capacity, with not a single place available where he could sit. Outside the hall, there was a room where all the invitees had left their shoes. Sant Tulsidas went and sat in the midst of shoes.

Can you imagine the scene? Sant Tulsidas, a saint who belonged to a high caste, the author of the most beloved work on Sri Rama, actually sat in the midst of shoes! When food was distributed, Sant Tulsidas received it in a shoe and was about to eat it when a devotee recognised him and cried out, "Sant Tulsidas is here!" Immediately word spread that the great saint had arrived. Naabhaji, too, heard of it. He rushed to the place and was surprised to see the humility of Sant Tulsidas. He immediately escorted the saint to his guru, Swami Ugradas, who greeted him with humility and love.

Sant Tulsidas and Swami Ugradas sat besides each other and both were served the *langar* by Naabhaji with great reverence.

Is not humility the one essential mark of every true saint? Many of us are egoistic. Small accomplishments make us feel proud. We regard ourselves as superior to others. A little wealth, a little power, a little prestige, a little beauty – and we are apt to imagine that we are better than the best! But youth and wealth and beauty are transient. They soon pass away! Today, they may be with us, tomorrow, they vanish in the vast!

Humility is a mark of every true devotee, of every sincere *bhakta* of the Lord. For, he believes that he is only an instrument, a broken instrument through whom God chooses to do his work of help and healing.